The Heart
of
My Soul

The Heart
of
My Soul

TALES OF FIVE GENERATIONS
AT THE FAMILY CABIN

Janet Kurtz

To request permission, contact the publisher at:
        publisher@innerpeacepress.com

ISBN: 978-1-958150-37-5
The Heart of My Soul: Tales of Five Generations at the Family Cabin

First publication: October 2024

All photos and illustrations courtesy of Janet Kurtz.

Published by **Inner Peace Press**
Eau Claire, Wisconsin, USA
www.innerpeacepress.com

Dedicated to and in memory of:

My mother, Phyllis M. (Wise) Kurtz
and my father, Donald W. Kurtz

Gratitude and eternal love for the foundations
you provided for my brother, Steven, and for me,
raising us to be mindful of our Mother Earth
and all of its inhabitants.

Yes, Mom, it should have been a clue,
when your date stopped to pick up that
road kill raccon and took it home for supper.

Dad, in your defense,
your ecology, your respect for
Natural Law, your vast abilities
to preserve, provide, and protect
our family, are duly noted.

Contents

Snippets

Come Sit with Me

Foreword
The Cabin

*T*his early April snow shower might dampen my spirit's journey into spring, but not snuff out the spark lit just last week. Then, the first robin, the first 70°F temperature, and the first bike ride around the lake, took me soaring into spring mode. It hit so hard that I flew past my spring-cleaning list right into my "opening the cabin" agenda.

The cabin that my father built with his father is now my inheritance. Dad plotted out the floor plan with strings in the backyard of his Illinois parsonage when I was a toddler. He and a college buddy bought the log cabin property in northern Wisconsin from Dr. Harr, their seminary professor, after a tornado swept over it. These two young ministers bushwhacked their way down the lane to the lake and decided to share the cabin between their two families. This arrangement dissolved when it became clear that the workload was not a coordinated vision.

My father, Don, set out to survey the acreage and came up with the only possible building spot, a steep hill leading to the lake on the east bay. A ledge was cut out with the old bulldozer. Horses were brought in to move the logs felled with cross-cut saws. The floor plan strings were laid out on the leveled shelf and building was begun with his father, Floyd, and a bevy of friends.

In the 1950s a lot of family cottages eked their way into existence. Meager wages led to scavenger hunts in lumber piles, windows from scrap yards, and second hand bricks. Grandpa Floyd was a bridge builder with engineering and cement expertise. Dad had learned carpentry along the way. They managed. The cabin was a work in progress until 2013, when my father dismantled the steps leading to the outdoor shower just three months before his death.

During his last few years, he questioned his decision to gift me the family cabin. Wouldn't it be a lot of headaches and maintenance? It has electricity and a phone, but the location between the creek and the lake never lent itself to a drain field and plumbing. The pump is six steps from the front door and the outhouse a one minute hike. The woodshed still protects enough split oaks and birch to last a decade.

Of course, I'll keep the family cabin. It seemed daunting, at first. My only brother, Steven, died in 1985. My son and his family only get about five days a year to go there. My husband's mantra is: *Been there, done that*. But, of course, I will be the guardian of the spot on earth that houses the spirits of my grandparents along with my memories of childhood.

There are the bear stories, like Auntie Wilma going totally in opposition to my Dad's "Bear Protocol" instructions. There are the fish stories, like when my son, Greg, and I caught that muskie "with our bare hands." There are new stories added by the most recent generation — my two grandkids, Ella and James. There are the mayfly and dragonfly hatches, the sucker runs, and the monarch butterflies. The "kid" pontoon that floated here 15 years ago after a storm, never to be claimed, finally had its bon voyage, making room for two new orange kayaks. Change.

The family cabin is an enigma to so many folks now pondering these relics of past generations. Are they museums filled with wood stoves, rocking chairs, two handled saws hanging from rafters, squeaky screen doors, and ghosts? Or, are they the gifts we will pass on to the next layer of family?

I am choosing door number two. I am choosing to take my dad's dream and "pay it forward." This genuine cottage has more than a past. I asked Russ, a local neighbor who helps when we are not there, to put in the dock and mow the trails again this year. That hand-made quilt we bought at the garage sale for $10.00 will be perfect in the guest room. Mom is already planning the menus!

This little April snow shower hasn't dampened my dreams of another summer at the cabin. It just rekindled the spark.

ACKNOWLEDGEMENTS

To all the players that walked through the woods, swam the waters, and gazed into the Milky Way, I thank you for your participation in these tales. That includes the beaver, despite damming the creek; the phoebes, even though you wake me at dawn; and the snake in my kayak for giving me that story.

To the humans, I am grateful to the five generations that created this niche on the hill, bringing character, care, and love to this space. May those who follow respect this ridge and the gifts of the planet.

Much gratitude to Heather Felty, the guru behind the scenes, supporting me through the emotions, the sinfin (endless) photos, the encouragement and the necessary technology to bring this together. Yikes! Such talent. I am deeply grateful.

Whether you are included in this book or not, please add your voice to the story!

~Janet E. Kurtz

Kurtz (Wise) Family Tree

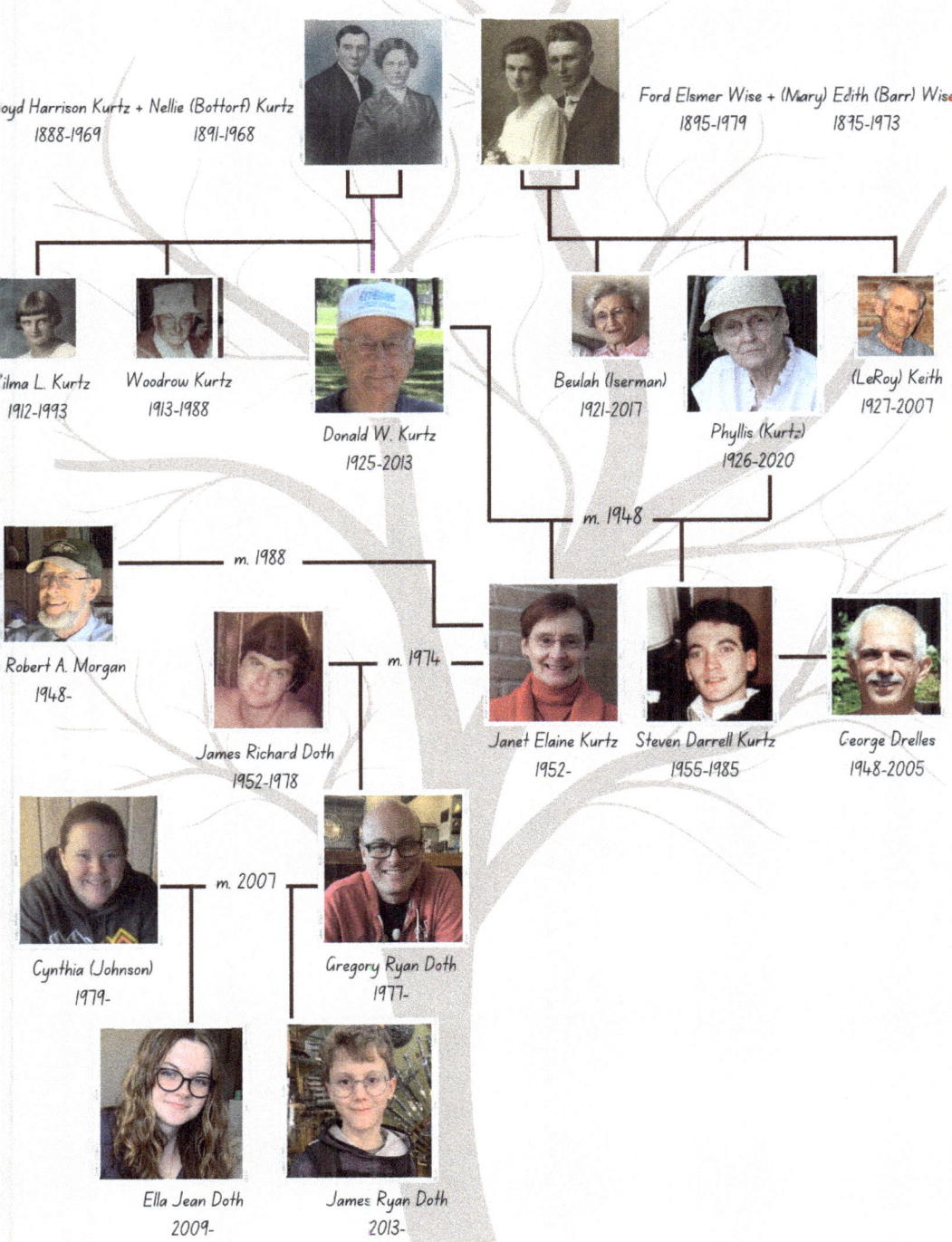

oyd Harrison Kurtz + Nellie (Bottorf) Kurtz
1888-1969   1891-1968

Ford Elsmer Wise + (Mary) Edith (Barr) Wise
1895-1979   1875-1973

ilma L. Kurtz
1912-1993

Woodrow Kurtz
1913-1988

Donald W. Kurtz
1925-2013

Beulah (Iserman)
1921-2017

Phyllis (Kurtz)
1926-2020

(LeRoy) Keith
1927-2007

m. 1948

m. 1988

Robert A. Morgan
1948-

James Richard Doth
1952-1978

m. 1974

Janet Elaine Kurtz
1952-

Steven Darrell Kurtz
1955-1985

George Drelles
1948-2005

Cynthia (Johnson)
1979-

m. 2007

Gregory Ryan Doth
1977-

Ella Jean Doth
2009-

James Ryan Doth
2013-

The Land

History
1863 to Present (2001)

Written by Donald W. Kurtz

*T*he land occupied by Donald and Phyllis Kurtz is traced through an abstract which records that the United States granted the State of Wisconsin on March 13, 1863.

The objective of the transfer of the land from the United States to the State of Wisconsin was to get a Military Road constructed between Fort Howard at Green Bay, Wisconsin, and Fort Wilkins at Copper Harbor, Michigan.

The State of Wisconsin divided its interest in the area to Charles Smith (1/4 interest), Amalon Crowell, (3/16 interest) and George Fletcher (9/16 interest). This transfer was done by contract in exchange for the commitment of these individuals to build a section of the Military Road.

On June 10, 1878, the above named three land holders negotiated for the land to become property of the Page and Landeck Lumber Company. On September 12, 1914, Page and Landeck became joint partners with a lumber company by the name of Dandeder and Mel.

On February 27, [1911], the particular Section and Range bordering Lake [Julia] was obtained by the Robbins Lumber Company. The Robbins Company disposed of the holdings bordering Lake Julia to the Thunder Lake Lumber Company on August 11, 1919.

The Thunder Lake Lumber Company released ownership August 10, 1932, to Dr. Irvin A. Koten, Battle Creek, Michigan. This was a completed transaction on April 11, 1933. On January 2, 1946, Dr. Koten, then a chemistry professor at North Central College at Naperville, Illinois, and wife, Dora, sold approximately 54 acres to Dr. Wilbur Harr and Juanita. Dr. Harr was a professor of Missions at the Evangelical Theological Seminary at Naperville, Illinois.

In 1951, the Harrs sold their land to Edward R. Zager and Donald Kurtz, and spouse (Phyllis Wise Kurtz), who were students at Seminary where Dr. Harr was a professor.

The Zager-Kurtz partnership was dissolved on August 23, 1957, with the Kurtz's receiving 22 acres of the 54 acres held in the partnership. A "woods cabin" construction was begun on the Kurtz 22 acres in 1957. The completion may occur sometime in the year 2001!

The daughter of Donald and Phyllis Kurtz, Janet, is a Spanish teacher with a major emphasis on Latin American Cultures. The name given to the Kurtz holdings on Lake Julia is "Las Sobras," translated from Spanish meaning "leftovers."

The "leftovers" title has grown from Mr. Kurtz's philosophy of conservatism. This translated means "use what is usable." If an item is worn, but usable, fix it and use it. The effort is made to keep from contaminating pristine countryside by the disposition of "usables" in collective dumps defacing the lands we aim to protect from "pollution."

Phyllis is a retired third grade teacher. Donald was a pastor for 15 years and a staff psychologist for 20 years before retiring. Janet teaches at Central Lakes College at Brainerd, Minnesota. Robert, Janet's husband, is an Assistant State Park Manager for the DNR at Crow Wing Park. Grandson, Gregory Doth, lives in St. Louis Park, MN. Deceased family members: Son-in-law, James R. Doth, 1978 (aged 25) and son, Steven Darrell Kurtz, 1985, Northwestern University School of Music (aged 30).

Lake Julia Property Journal 1999

Written by Donald W. Kurtz

The Kurtz Cabin was built in 1958 by Donald Kurtz. Most of the cabin and all of the boat house was constructed with lumber retrieved from structures dismantled by Mr. Kurtz. There is no sub-flooring beneath the regular flooring. There is no sheathing under the siding. All doors in the building are from dismantled dormitory buildings of a church camp. Paint was stripped after which stain was applied. The doors are covered with plywood to conceal damage to wood surface. "Storm" doors were purchased new. Insulation is 1-inch blanket except around the windows in the "dining-living room" which were installed in 1997 where 3-inch insulation was installed.

The floor joists are 2x8-inch spaced 30 inches apart instead of the usual standard width space. Floors have sagged toward the center from exterior walls to the walls separating the bedrooms from the dining-living room and the wall separating the porch and the dining-living room. The kitchen space floor tilts toward the porch sufficiently to permit a marble to move from a stand still to the porch wall. The roof to the north is dipped sufficiently to be visible from the ground outside. Roof rafters are full dimension 2x4-inch Red Pine lumber marketed by a saw-mill in Crandon in 1958. These rafters were used instead of the usual 2x6-inch dimension due to inadequate funds for purchasing the more standard rafters (unfortunately).

Ceilings in the bedrooms and part of the living-dining are pressed-wood left-over scraps from a manufacturer of overhead garage doors. The interior cedar paneling was sold by the lumber yard as "layout" pieces due to knots that were loosened or dropped out entirely. Paneling in the upstairs loft is material retrieved from discarded sections in dismantling elsewhere and then painting them.

The "boat house" is constructed by lumber from a dismantled garage and the siding covering the sheathing is from a house where it was removed (1920 Rudolph Rd., Eau Claire, WI) when vinyl siding was installed. The outhouse is from scraps also including the pressed wood from the discard from the door making manufacturer.

The land plot of 21.7 acres resulted in a "down the middle" division of North line footage of the original plot of land jointly purchased in 1951 by Edward Zager and his wife, Virginia, and Donald Kurtz and his wife, Phyllis. This "partnership" was dissolved in 1958. Mr. Kurtz began with nothing but the then unsurveyed land parcel of 21.7 acres. The solitary building site available was bulldozed level sufficient to build the structure as it stands in 1999.

The survey contracted for in 1987 by Mr. Kurtz revealed an irregular and elongated shoreline of approximately 1155 feet of comparison to the North "back" line of 975.43 feet. This "shoreline" consists of 369 feet of wetland/swamp to the east of the cabin. To the west of this, where the cabin stands, there is 200 feet of usable shorefront to dock and/or remove small boats or canoes. This type of shoreline ends 20 feet west of the boathouse.

A ridge rises from the water level to the ridge between 35-60 feet all the way to the west line of the property. The angle of incline to the water is about 60 degrees and the distance covered is about 586 feet. The easement road to the Franke (formerly Zager) property to the west crosses this property on the north side of the ridge and rises gradually alongside the ridge until reaching the top of the ride of the Franke (Zager) property. This easement further narrows the depth of the high ground on the Kurtz Property.

A creek runs through the 21.7 acre property and the bottom land of the creek is all wetland and bog, requiring rubber boots, particularly in the wet season. These observations presumably leaves approximately 8-10 acres of solid ground on the plot.

At the cabin, the water supply comes from a driven sand-point to a depth of 25 feet. The building area is not conducive to a holding tank for a septic system. A pumping tank truck cannot enter the area through the lane due to truck size. The lane access is over U.S. Forest Service land. Mr. Kurtz pays the government an annual fee for easement and is required to maintain the former logging trail for transport. This lane covers a half mile to the gate on the Kurtz property beginning at the end of Hillside Road where the government placed a gate and earthen embankment to prohibit "all-wheelers" from eroding the hills of the old Sheltered Valley Ski Hill.

At the cabin, "graywater" is disposed of outside. Water supply is maintained in pails. The "outhouse" serves as the toilet.

The original louver windows in the cabin are opened with a crank. Several of the cranks are no longer functional, making window opening and closing impossible. The only construction improvements to the cabin have been a skylight window and the picture windows at living/dining room space. The windows replaced louver windows that were no longer operable.

Compiled June 25, 1999
(Signed)
Donald W. Kurtz

The Esker

The glacier did it. It left this great big pile of soil, rocks, and refuse right here. Way back, maybe 10,000 years or more, the glacier stopped here and melted. The 10,000 years comes from a sign a few miles down the road, explaining that the marsh was once a lake and the bogs dated to that time period. I'm taking that observation and applying it to this ridge.

The ridge is a sort of hump, rising up in the middle, both sides swooping down the esker's banks, one into the lake and the other into the connecting creek. The ridge slopes down to the peninsula, now called "The Point." The Point is where the palisade cabin was first built in the 1940s, with a surrounding view of the lake and the creek flowing in from the bogs.

I heard once that the Native Americans (indigenous people) view eskers as sacred, and I've adopted that belief. The massive image of a glacier moving over the land and stopping here impresses me. People in the gravel pit business view this differently.

This day, and innumerable other afternoons throughout my life, I have the privilege of sitting on the esker's edge, where it meets the lake. Growing up, my parents would sit here with my brother and me, looking up into the sky, watching for the clouds appearing over the treetops. The parade of shape-shifting clouds inspired our imaginations.

Like now. Just moments ago, I was in my big innertube under a wall-to-wall blue sky. Then, a celestial popcorn popper spit little white clouds into sight. I watched one lengthen into a full-grown girl with ponytail, her nose jutted out and lips puckered. Another cloud grew to meet her, nearly as tall, but with the ears of a rabbit – a jack rabbit. I could see his thumper feet. He reached across the sky to kiss her before stretching out into thin air.

Now the popcorn kernels are being blown by an ominous wind, rising over the esker and bending the tallest pines eastward, the blue sphere covering with shades of grey, changing the color of the water below to wavy lines of black.

How quickly the sky and my moods change. How quickly the years pass. How long will the esker be sacred after I no longer sit here and watch the clouds float over?

One day the esker will likely still be here edging the lakeshore, her grasses still bowing in the breezes. The chipmunk will likely still scold. Hopefully, monarchs will still flit between the milkweed. Perhaps, like 10,000 years ago, there will not be people roosting on her back, nor artificial waves from their motor crafts crashing against her shore. Perhaps, people will have squandered their chance to hold her sacred.

Meet Donald, 2006

Written by Donald W. Kurtz

*M*y life is remembered by behaviors that grew within me due to my parents, teachers, and friends. My early memories involve planting a garden for the first time at age five. Carrots, radishes, onions, and lettuce were placed in about a nine-square-foot plot next to the large family garden that consisted of cabbage, corn, potatoes, and squash. The crops kept us fed year around in the 1930s.

Every task was demonstrated to me. Performing the job immediately followed, whether it was spading the ground, splitting wood, digging potatoes, picking corn, or gathering eggs in the chicken house nests. Eggs were often traded by the dozen for bananas, oranges, apples, etc. Survival meant working for what you received and being careful with what one did.

Father, Floyd, was a bridge builder/cement contractor. He graduated from grade school at age 16, because boys only went to classes from November to March while during the other months, they worked at crops on the family farm or milked 4-10 cows twice a day by hand — stripping out about 2½ gallons from each animal.

At age 17, Floyd was accepted into college in Iowa and got a general engineering degree in less than two years in 1908. He married Nellie Loretta Bradley Bottorf. Nellie was a cook, seamstress, piano player, flower gardener, vegetable gardener, and raised canary birds. She was orderly and strict. Everything was to have a place and kept there. No clutter.

Father was a role-model teaching his children arithmetic, book keeping, mechanics, use of tools, wrenches, hammers, and saws. We used everything. Nothing was wasted. When clothes could not be patched further, they were braided into rugs. Boards were bought full sized and were cut to fit where needed, and eventually projects surfaced where pieces were utilized. As scraps developed, they were used in the fire at the furnace or laundry stove. Construction, at that time, was not done after freezing weather developed all day long.

Time was then used to cut firewood in the woodlands. Dammed up creeks created ice ponds where small town residents cut blocks of ice, which were stored in sawdust piles for summer use in ice boxes. Food was kept from spoiling in the ice boxes until freezing weather returned. The blocks thawed to about half of the original size that they were in February by the time October returned.

People were considerably more respectful of God and Jesus in this era. Nobody worked on Sunday. Many went to worship. The day of rest was time for thought. Great respect was given to ones' blessings, enabling the continuance of life. As time progressed after World War II, people seemed to become more greedy and less respectful of others. Some felt like rugs being walked on, or ladders for others to climb to the top of mountains of money.

Fortunately, there were those still surviving who respected God-given resources. These people possess vision of when waste and greed lead all things in living creation. As I write this on my resting back, on the porch of the Julia Lake cabin, there are countless memories of people who helped freely with their labors and collected "fees" by later coming for free to stay in this "Garden of Eden."

As one looks at the cabin, its furnishings, its structure, its contents, it is obvious there is not comparison of quality or style to 2006 condominiums, townhouses, etc. Daughter of Phyllis and

Donald Kurtz, Janet, is a super person in her knowledge of Spanish, which she teaches with other Latin American courses. Her motto for this building site and lake front is "Las Sobras."

In 2006, looking at this building causes questions about how long will it serve living purposes for residents. My religion, among other things, requires me not to waste God's material gifts. Questions can be legitimately raised as to whether time used to utilize leftovers is well spent or could other employment have been more outreaching, helpful, and productive. At this point, it is too late to do anything retrieving about life that may have been better used.

I do take some joy in not having destroyed these renewable gifts, as given by the Creator. Unlike what you see as you travel mile after mile across this country. I fashioned this place to honor the Native Americans, who consumed only necessary animal and plant life to survive in a territory of beauty and abundance.

From a leftover – among many others,
Donald W. Kurtz

Don, The Dreamer

The Story of Two Cabins

by Donald Kurtz
excerpt from 1993 letter to new owners

*D*onald Kurtz and Edward Zager purchased approximately 54 acres in 1951 while still enrolled in Seminary at Naperville, Illinois. The purchase was made from Dr. Wilbur C. Harr, Naperville, Illinois. Dr. Harr was Missions Professor at the Evangelical Theological Seminary. He had conducted mission efforts in central Africa.

Dr. Harr had acquired the property from Dr. Irvin Koten who was head of the chemistry department at North Central College at Naperville, Illinois. Dr. Koten was the father of Donald Koten who, as of this date, owns the acreage on the south side of the Lake Julia area surrounding the bay south of the island. Don Koten is a professor in forestry at Syracuse University, in Syracuse, New York. Dr. Koten, at one time, was owner of 78 acres now owned by the Ringenoldus family, 54 acres sold to Dr. Harr and the 90 acres presently occupied by Don Koten (some of the 90 acres has been sold).

The cabin built by Dr. Wilbur Harr was re-arranged to provide a "duplex" of sorts with two kitchen areas and one "neutral" bedroom that was used by the particular resident at a given time.

The Kurtz–Zager partnership dissolved in 1957 after deliberation over the means of division. A decision was made to divide the 54 acres at the half-way point of the north line which resulted in the Kurtz's receiving approximately 22 acres and the Zager's approximately 33 acres. The land had not been surveyed except by "chaining."

Allocation of cabin contents was made. Some remuneration was made by Zager to Kurtz making it possible for the Kurtz' to have a building site bulldozed from a side hill, establishing a well and beginning structure of other necessary buildings.

On a salary of about $2,000 annually, the building of a cottage, equipping furnishings, and keeping a passable road without car muffler damage was difficult. Vacation time was limited to two weeks annually. In 1957, the Kurtz's took a year's leave of absence from serving the denomination at Dwight, Illinois, in what is now known as the United Methodist Church. Residence in Three Lakes, Wisconsin, was arranged by "Cy" Williams, who was a former Cub baseball star and graduate architect from Purdue University. Cy designed and built the Northernaire and, among many other buildings, churches, civic buildings, and the Sheltered Valley Ski Hill Lodge, made of logs.

Donald Kurtz worked for Cy that year during the daytime and worked on the "cottage" at night. The salary was $1.50 per hour. Donald Kurtz's father had been a builder of bridges and other concrete construction. Wages were supplemented while in Three Lakes by serving a congregation in Phelps, Wisconsin, on an interim basis and by working for the Forest Service for four of the winter months.

At the original Point Cabin, 1955

Ed and Ginnie Zager with Peggy and Judy   Phyllis and Donald with baby Janet

Memories

Point Cabin as it looked when Zagers and Kurtz' arrived in 1951

Janet and Steven with Grandpa Floyd, 1956

Phyllis takes Janet wading at the Point Cabin, 1954

Grandma Nellie, at the Point Cabin, 1956

Steven and Janet Kurtz, 1955, in the former bed used by their father - present day woodbox

The Construction
More Leftovers

Written by Donald W. Kurtz

The Lake Julia cabin and land is the central collection of innumerable memories of people and of origins of building supplies, which we describe the cabin as "Las Sobras."

Floyd Kurtz, my father, loaned me money through a promissory note with no interest and no term deadline. Pay off was made, however, in about two years. After six years of co-ownership, the wise move for the future seemed to be to dissolve partnership, divide the acreage, and I would build my own cabin with little or no money.

Money was extremely scarce. My first year's salary at work in 1951 was $1,900. There were many helpful friends for which my blessings are recalled almost with guilty conscience and wonderment, "what have I ever done to deserve this?" Lumber was bought only as it was affordable. Frame lumber, siding, and flooring came from a sawmill near Crandon. Cedar paneling was "layout" quality, because of loose or missing knots. Those were eliminated by sawing off and discarding defective areas.

The cabin frame was in Norway pine. The sheathing or the roof is white pine. The tongue-and-groove flooring is fir in the living room, dining room, and kitchen. The porch and bedrooms are tongue-and-groove yellow pine. None of the lumber cost more than $100 per one thousand feet. Some cost as little as $60 per thousand board feet.

The out-house is made of pressed fiber materials which is left-over from door manufacturing firm from Bureau Company, Illinois. These pieces also were used to cover the ceilings in the cabin. All pieces were 11 inches or narrower and 12 foot lengths.

Three chests of drawers were made for bedrooms from leftover pieces of ¼-inch plywood. The only tools used were a square, a handsaw, and a hammer. The bed frames were constructed from white birch "logs" from the woods and 2x4 pieces as a base for the mattress. Furniture pieces are mostly a collection of cast-offs. An "Eagle Claw" living room table originated in a garage of cast-offs to be taken to the dump.

An oak desk was purchased in 1950 for $2.50 from a classmate in college. The market currently offers $200 to $250 for similar piece. A glass door library shelf of oak is something from around the 1900s. A coffee table of maple is also an antique purchase at an antique store in Crandon.

The dining room table, chairs, and buffet are Duncan Phyfe style of walnut furniture and was sold to us for $50 by a physician at our first pastoral assignment. The "game shelf" was made by Mrs. Wilbur Harr, the wife of the professor who sold us the property in 1951. Two chairs were retrieved from the old Sheltered Ski-hill lodge. The building was increasingly entered after its closure and many pieces of classic furniture were smashed. After about three visits to the lodge, I took an arm chair and dinner table chair to the cabin before they were all smashed and trashed. I felt rewarded when, on the next "visit" there was not a single intact piece of furniture left.

A table of maple furnishes the porch's "lunch center." These items came from a renter on our property who left the table in broken but fixable condition.

The "wood box" was one used by my grandparents and parents in the 1920s and 1930s. Before I had a full-sized bed, the "woodbox" served as a "bed" for me during early pre-school times – ages 1-3! Next to the wood box is an antique wash stand that my parents had received from one of their parents (my grandparents). This became my property in 1993. There were broken shelves and a marred top, which was fixed by using some 5/4 (five quarter) boards salvaged from some throwaway lumber.

The three bedroom doors are old maple, which had been made available to me by the Oakdale Church Camp, south of Freeport, Illinois. An old wooden dormitory was demolished and I got the doors covered with several layers of paint. When the paint was removed, the natural pine was beautifully grained.

The front door is an old door covered with pieces of leftover plywood. The picture of a man and his dog on a smokey window glass was left behind by another renter who left it at the rental house when he moved.

The back door is an old screen door covered with plywood. A window was inserted and secured in the upper half of the door. The porch windows separating the porch and living room are old barn windows, cut down to fit between the studs.

The only new items in the cabin are the refrigerator, the gas stove, the brick-lined wood burning stove, the bathroom sink, the clothes closet, and the towel cabinet.

Two minor items of significance are the "night" stand in one bedroom, which originally was part of a large bedroom dresser...

(I think he went to sleep, as penmanship got smaller, then a line of ink went down the page. JK)

Family Sayings from Five Generations

Floyd Kurtz:
"Load your truck, both coming and going."

Nellie Kurtz:
"A place for everything and everything in its place."

Don Kurtz:
"Act in haste, repent in leisure."

Janet Kurtz:
"Put the big rocks in first."

Greg Doth:
"How is that working out for you?"

Ella Doth:
"Shake things up a little. Do it for the plot."

The Guest Book
A Tradition

I believe the tradition of Guest Books came out of my father's profession as a pastor. He was called upon to "marry people' — a term that takes a second to comprehend. As a child, I often heard him say he was "going to marry" someone or he already had "married them" leading to my befuddlement regarding my mother.

The amount of wedding ceremonies came with the unspoken yet required tradition of gift giving. This young pastor and his wife were brought up to give gifts, but their budget called for intentional and equal giving. Thus, the Guest Book. It was thoughtful for the newlyweds starting out their new homes. It was reasonably priced and usually tasteful. With that, when the cabin opened to company, it came with a Guest Book.

Over the years, visitors went from signing to adding addresses, but most telling were the comments reminding us of highlights and the addition of actual electric lights. When the bird lists and tall tales of muskies entered in, the Guest Book was accompanied by The Cabin Journal. The tomes filled with photos, rough drawings, poems, menus, family quotes, and phenology.

If science is interested, we have volumes of weather reports, lists of bird sightings, sizes of muskies and snapping turtles, lake water levels, and the last time a whip-poor-will was heard. The tattered pages reveal personalities and release emotions. The years pass and so do the visitors.

Here is a photo of the first entries starting on August 12, 1957. The first to sign were Donald's parents, Floyd and Nellie, registered as Mr. and Mrs. F. H. (Floyd Harrison) Kurtz. I'll have to see if women ever signed in alone or when they stopped using "Mrs." with their husband's first name, thus fading totally into the shadows. So much to learn from Guest Books!

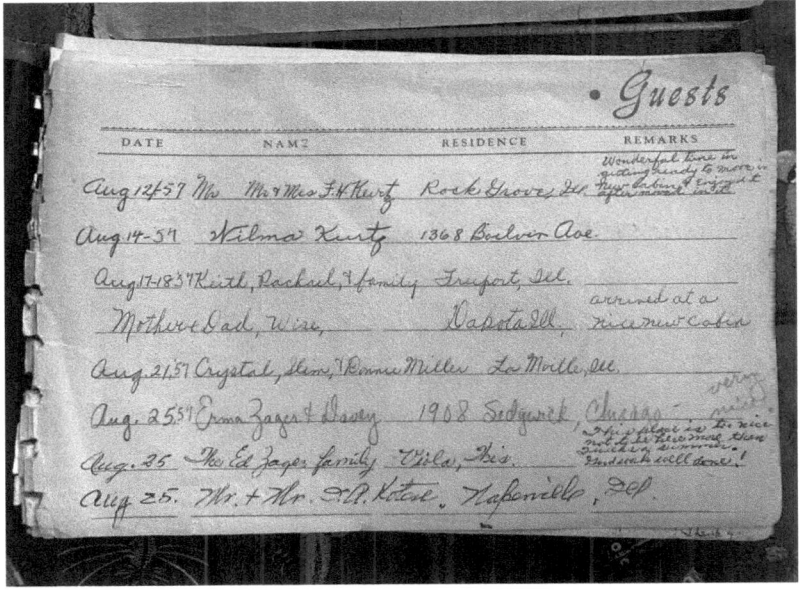

"This place is too nice not to be here more than 2 weeks a summer. Good work well done!"
– The Ed Zager family, August 25, 1957

Cabin 10 Commandments

*T*hou shalt ...

1) Fill the water pails... (pump gently)
2) Empty the chamber pot... (or reap consequences)
3) Stay seated in the boat... (especially when fishing)
4) Wear your life-preserver... (always: on dock, shoreline, always)
5) Be on time for meals...
   (don't keep the cook waiting or let food get cold)
6) Rest after lunch... (one hour minimum before swimming)
7) Take matches on walks... (bears are afraid of fire)
8) Wear light colors and long pants in tick season...
   (tuck pants into socks)
9) Bring in an armload of wood when passing by the woodshed...
   (supply chain)
10) Pack it in; pack it out... (be good stewards)

Donald Kurtz breaking the third commandment

Memories

Grandpa Floyd doing the block work, 1956   Framing up, 1956

Ford Wise, Wilma Kurtz, Floyd Kurtz, and Edith Wise working on the cabin, 1957

Cabin kitchen and dining area, 1957

Steven making popcorn in the kitchen, 1964

39

Meet the Matriarch
Phyllis (Wise) Kurtz

Mom's Point of View
The Other Side of the Story

The cabin entered their lives as the result of a tornado. Dr. Harr, a North Central professor had land and a palisade style log cabin. The winds blew. The trees fell down. His search for clean-up volunteers amongst his students fell on very attentive ears, especially of my father, Don, and his friend, Ed. They were bit by their imaginations, sans the input of their young wives.

The journey from Chicago, Illinois, to the rugged cabin at the end of an unimproved logging trail joined two entirely different planets. In 1951 there were no freeways, the cars lacked four-wheel drive, the hours were long, and toddlers were involved. When I asked mom for her first impressions, the events remained vivid as she sputtered out phrases:

"Horrible! I expected something like the cottages — at the Northernaire — like the ones my Aunt Thera stayed at when she brought Reggie up to help his asthma in the summer."

"With every mile out of Three Lakes, we were going back in time! Like a tunnel, taking us further and further away from civilization!"

"The logging trail was awful! We got stuck on a hill going in. It was 4:00 a.m. Just horrid!"

"When Nellie heard about our moving to Three Lakes, she cried her eyes out. Her son was leaving Dwight, Illinois, and his job as a minister to do *this*? She was so proud of her minister son. Nellie and Wilma thought your dad had lost his marbles. How could he move so far away? He was going to a god-forsaken wilderness."

"Floyd lent some money for the purchase and we packed belongings in his trailer. We dropped you two kids off at Grandma Edith's. Steve got sick but Mom didn't take him to Dr. Powers. Steve had strep throat. I was so far away."

"Yup, I was totally against this, in every way."

"But your dad already had a job with Cy Williams. The rental house had saggy floors and thin walls. Nellie was livid. She'd say, 'Darn stubborn Kurtz was going to go ahead and do what he wanted.' She and Floyd had loud disagreements that often invoked the 'stubborn Kurtz' or 'stubborn German' equivalent."

The other side of the story. The woman's side. My mom (and later I) joined those historical pioneering women, packing dreams into a Conestoga wagon leaving civilization in the dust. Dreams for one can be nightmares for another. Along the way, it works out, but not before some hopes and expectations fall to the wayside. In the end, Mom savored the peace, the wild things, and made memories with the company sitting around her table. Her story?

Sometimes, she held the memories in her heart and other times, she held her tongue when it came to: The family cabin.

Her dream: The Northernaire
Her reality: A remote cabin five miles away
Phyllis Kurtz visiting her Aunt on Big Stone, 1940s

Cursive and Exclamation Points!

The hand-writing on the envelope has not changed in over 80 years. It is a practiced, flowing cursive, decorative in its capital letters and fully formed lowercased vowels. On the inside stationery, the alphabet comes together in groups of adjectives describing Sunday's church service with references to attendees, who stayed for coffee, and a summation of the sermon. And always, always a review of the music.

"The choir was absolutely marvelous!" she writes. "There were thirty-four singing this week. They did a cantata. Remember meeting the grandson of my friend, Mary? The one who is studying to be in opera? He did a solo and was amazing! It is just bliss to listen to him! He is so talented! We are lucky to have him!" The exclamation marks march across the page.

She lives her days in surprise and wonder. Every day after she's finished the daily crosswords, her balance exercises, cutting out a new recipe from the newspaper, and reading her latest book, she calls me.

"Janet, I have been reading the best book!" she begins, using the name she gave me at birth.

"I just can't believe all I am learning about our government! Can this all be true? I mean, I lived through World War II and thought we were, what shall I say, that we were above corruption and government manipulation. This story about the Supreme

Court rulings is such an eye-opener! We need more women. And," she pauses for emphasis, "term limits on some of those guys!" Exclamation point.

Maybe she was always like this, but I have noticed it more since Dad died five years ago. She grew up in northern Illinois, with its rural, god-fearing, farm-centered, neighborly-like, community-minded, flag-respecting cosmology. As she sits on her flower-patterned couch in the warmth of her condo sunroom, she seems to be blossoming, finding her voice.

The 9/11 attack on the Twin Towers challenged her world view. Instead of joining in the litany of fear and ignorance, she went to the library and returned home with collections on Islam, Saudi Arabia, Afghanistan, and Al-Qaeda. After 70 years, her politics changed as she gasps her way through *Fire and Fury* by Michael Wolff, *A Warning* by Anonymous, and *FEAR* by Bob Woodward. Occasionally she still tunes in to hear Rush Limbaugh's side.

"Janet, I believe it is important to get both sides, but now I can only manage about 15 minutes," she said, turning off the radio during my last visit.

I live four hours away. Winter weather is a travel factor. Summer's long daylight hours offer more relaxed drives. Regardless, I need my regular doses of Mom.

"Are you going to be here for lunch?" she always, always asks.

"It depends on when I get out of here." I always, always answer.

I leave home when it gets light out. The miles allow me to adjust from my life of wood fires and foraging turkey flocks to join her afternoon "book-teas" when she serves cherry chocolate chip cookies and lays out her latest tomes on the bed for friends to peruse and borrow.

Or, she schedules in local events. "Janet, do you want me to sign you up for the Prime Time lunch? It's a presentation by the church members that went to the immigrant conference in Nogales last month. And there is a JONAH meeting on migrants Tuesday, if you can stay."

I drive the miles and call her when I'm closer, so she can heat up lunch. When I arrive, the dining room table is covered with the china from my wedding that I never used. The silverware is silver from her wedding. The cloth napkins are rolled inside the brightly colored ceramic rings I bought in Mexico. The tablecloth was hand-painted by Luisa, one of my Argentine exchange teachers. There are individual salt and pepper shakers at each plate.

"Now, let's pray before I bring out the food. I know you like it hot."

We embrace, shut our eyes, and she begins.

"Thank you, Creator God, for this food, our shelter, our friends, and our family. Thank you for Janet's safe journey here. We are thankful for our health and our many blessings. Be with those less fortunate. Amen."

She empties the pans of food into serving dishes used by her mother, even though they will again be empty the moment we serve ourselves. I will be on my third bite of salmon, a new recipe, when she begins to review dessert options. She's already anticipating the chocolate in her future.

I watch her and realize the world is missing something special by not trying out new recipes served on good china in the middle of the week. "Use your good stuff," she admonishes, "What are you waiting for?"

I treasure her habits, her delight in blue birds, glee over getting a maraschino cherry on her ice cream sundae, despair over politics, and, now, her third-grade-teacher-self rears up at the newspaper's headline. "What? They want to drop cursive writing from the elementary curriculum!"

Today, another letter arrived with her familiar cursive penmanship. I tear it open and read, "I'm going to make a peach pie when that Georgia truck comes to town tomorrow!"

What a loss to future generations, if these nuggets of personal exclamations cannot be read.

May 30, '90

Dear Janet, Greg, & Robert,

It's been another beautiful day. The sky is so blue & not a cloud in it! The grass & leaves are so green — must look like Ireland!

When I awoke today, I wondered what I'd do. But it all worked out. We had Ed for lunch, so that gave me something to do in the A.M. After lunch, he & Don experimented calling back & forth to check on our phone. It "gurgled" instead of ringing. Don sanded the points & taped a broken wire & now it rings, but has a gurgling echo.

I wanted to hike the Thunder Lake railroad trail this P.M. & Don thought I might get lost so he went, too. Ed drove us to a point & dropped us off & we walked back to the cabin — a distance of 4½ miles. It took 2 hours. It was lovely to be out.

Rompecabezas
Mom's Crossword Habit

"What is the word for 'week' in Oaxaca?" she hollers out to me from the living room couch.

"*Semana*," I answer back from the cabin kitchen. "Does *semana* fit? It is the Spanish word, but maybe they are looking for an indigenous one?"

"Well, *semana* fits, but that means I have to change my answer for number six across. Maybe you are wrong?" she infers.

When it comes to Spanish, it is the one time I have right answers in crossword puzzles. I taught the language my entire career. Still, she hesitates.

"Is there a key in the back of your book?" I ask, to which she nods in the affirmative. "Ok then, let me have a look," I offer. "That way you won't peek at the other answers."

I take the book and check. "Aha," I say with self-satisfaction, "*Semana* it is. Guess you'll have to use your eraser."

I return to the task of washing dishes, something she usually does these days. Ever since the skin cancer test came back positive, her usual outdoor activities have to fit before or after the 10:00-2:00 sun-time hours, rescheduling her reading, cooking, and crosswords.

Me? I'm always anxious to get back outside. After seven days of rain, I am thrilled to see the sunshine return. I pick up the laundry basket and move toward the door. I notice her head is slightly bobbing to her chest, pencil falling from her relaxing hand. According to her, she never naps, but just "rests" her eyes.

Suddenly, the out-of-order phone shatters our wilderness quiet. She levitates off the couch before I can catch the second ring.

"What, what...?" she blearily mutters.

"Seems like the phone company fixed the lines. Just go back to your, um... crosswords," I urge.

She looks down at the page, retrieves her pencil, puts the tip to her tongue and asks, "Do you know anything about this 'Jay-Lay' word? It comes up in so many puzzles."

"Spell that please. Doesn't sound like anything I ever heard of before."

She slowly spells out: "J a i – a l a i."

"Oh, *jai alai*. That is pronounced 'high – lie' in Spanish. It is a ball game. The fastest ball game in the world," I finish, loving the fact I know something.

"How did you know that?" she asks. "I thought it was French."

"From my Spanish textbook cultural notes. Think of all the space we would have left in our brains if it weren't full of all this trivia!"

"Like trying to remember the name of that horse," she referred back to our morning conversation, "that horse in the movie. I knew it started with an 'S' but it wasn't Stewball. Then, it came to me. Sea Biscuit! Why would I remember that and not people's names at church?"

I had heard her mention this aging malady before. I knew my day was coming. However, in the present moment, I remembered the laundry.

"Bring the clothes to me when they're dry and I'll iron," she called after me. "I need to get up off this couch."

"That will be a while," I said, still balancing the basket of wet clothes on my hip.

She leans back into her throw pillows, again touches the pencil tip to her tongue, and calls out to me as I open the door to leave. "What is a six-letter word for a city on the Costa del Sol?"

"Málaga, Mom. It's a port town with a view. Not touristy like Torremolinos. Anyway, Torremolinos is too many letters." I shift the clothesbasket and, just as the screen door is about to slap shut behind me, I hear her exclaim:

"M-a-l-a-g-a? It fits!"

"But," she pauses and adds, "I'll have to see if it works with my other words."

Pressing Matters

Published in *The Talking Stick,* vol. 26, 2017
Jackpine Writers' Bloc Inc., Menahga, MN

"What are you doing crawling across the top of the bed?" I asked my 90-year-old mother as she pulled the sheet toward the opposite side. "It's a tight squeeze, but you can walk around the edge."

"I'm lining up the stripes," she replied. "It's really easy with this pattern to just line them up."

"Why do they need to be lined up?" I asked, perplexed.

"So that I can sleep better at night."

"But, your eyes will be shut," I pointed out while leaning over to help line up the last set of stripes on my side.

"True. But, I will know," she smiled sweetly.

"Is this like your habit of hanging up clothes by color and size?"

She patted down the bedspread, crawled back across, and slid off the bed as she explained.

"It's artistic. I love to hang up clothes. Our condo ought to allow clotheslines. Why, kids these days don't even know the smell of freshly aired laundry!" She bemoaned yet another loss to the most recent generation born on earth.

"Well, I guess they'll never know the love of ironing, either," I added. "Remember the time you ironed my underpants? Sheets maybe, but underwear?"

She threw me a pseudo-scowl. "I like to iron. Besides having stripes lined up, I like to sleep on ironed sheets. And, I like them to fit. Not like the queen-sized ones on my regular bed at home. It's such a struggle to tuck them in, but at least they don't wrinkle. You see, I have cut back on ironing," she said as if vindicated.

"Ok, you're improving," I conceded, "But, how about the habit of counting things? Remember the time you counted all the paddle strokes when we canoed back from Virgin Lake to Julia?"

"It's uninhabited wilderness. I did it to pass the time," she said, then added, "Plus, I wanted to know."

"But, Mom, you counted for one and a half hours," I protested. "I was enjoying the white lilies, turtles, eagles, and..."

"That was a long time ago," she interrupted. I laughed, unconvinced.

"Hey, Mom," I said, changing the subject. "How about we go berry picking? Maybe we'll find enough for breakfast."

I grabbed two berry boxes, "Ya coming?"

Walking along the lane, we spied some raspberry bushes and plucked a few remaining tiny berries. The pickings were slim. She peered into my box and squealed, "That's not OK! You have more than I do!"

"We could count them," I offered with a grin.

"Exactly what I was thinking," she smirked. "How 'bout we just put them together and go fix breakfast."

At breakfast, she placed two dishes of berries on the table.

"There," she said, "I combined them."

"Good job, Mom," I said. "Now, we'll both get our fair share."

"Of course, we will. I counted them."

More from the Wise Side

At the end of every cabin stay, Phyllis was on a mission to clean up all the food. This haiku, written by her great-grandaugter Ella in summer 2024, encapuslates the sentiment:

> These are some nice buns
> They are not getting any younger
> We better eat them

As a teacher, Phyllis picked up a saying from her uncle Glen Wise, who used it in his classes and was remembered by generations of students:

"Every day we know more and more
About less and less
Until one day,
We'll know everything
About nothing at all!"

Seen on the classroom wall by the clock:

Time passes.
Will you?

Family Dynamics

Swish, swash, swish, swash, my father rounded the corner of the cabin carrying his full pail of water from the pump.

Right, left, right, left, his feet shuffle toward the screen door. Screeeech. It opened. Snap. It shut.

Swish, splash, groan, he hoists the white, enamel pail up to the counter and scooches it over to the spot where the dipper hangs on a hook. He is bent more by his years than the weight of the load that he carries.

It is an elongated space of a summer's day, which lazily fills with an unhurried lurch and its companion afternoon nap. It is August. The day has not yet made up its mind which way it will go. Will the next gust of wind bring down some rain or finally open up the clouds and let some hot sun shine sparkles on the waves? With each shift my inner pendulum swings from heading to the porch window seat with a novel or trotting to the lake with the inner tube and flippers. The sun goes under a cloud. My mood shifts again.

Clip, clop, his flip flops drag along the well-worn wooden floor to the south porch. There, he dips some water into a metal basin, squeezes the rough soap between his hands for a quick scrub, rinses, and reaches for the threadbare towel. He turns back into the cabin, calling over his shoulder that he is headed to the recliner. The window seat is free.

We are slowing down our speed as our week together comes to an end. Soon, Mom will leave to pick up her 89-year-old sister for a "girls' week" alone, back home.

Her cabin schedule starts with "five fruits" and oatmeal, brushing teeth, washing dishes, at which point we all go our own way until she rings the lunch bell, calling us back from the woods and water. Mom is the cook and preserver of social mores, which quickly fall apart once she leaves. This week, her leftovers will become our main menus. We have mashed potatoes, with rutabagas, grilled chicken, spinach salad with homemade dressing, and blackberry cobbler (berries she hand-picked), contained in various Tupperware.

"Eat up," she exclaims. "I hate all those little containers cluttering the fridge. Don't want to pack that in the cooler to go," she reminds us even as we are making a grocery list for next week.

Before leaving, Mom always does the wash. She loves to hang clothes up on the outdoor lines. This she does with artistic precision according to colors and size. It is a cabin tradition to have all the sheets clean, for next time. So, the day before she leaves, she sets up the ironing board on the porch, for the breeze and lake view, then irons all the sheets and pillowcases.

Her suitcase is packed light, as an old bathing suit, shorts, T-shirts, and a pair of patched workpants stay put in her dresser drawers. Dad stays clear of her while she makes her final inventory of the grounds. Last, she takes the Cabin Journal, sits by the east window, and writes:

"Saw the loons. Road repaired after deluge. Garden washed out over the bank in the big rainstorm. I will certainly miss the beans and lettuce. Narrowly escaped death by ladder when the wind blew it on me while weeding the flowers along the west side of cabin. Lake temperature is like bathwater. Not good for the fish." She finishes by sketching a color pencil portrait of herself floating in the big inner tube, then looks over at me.

"I think there is enough of your Dad's food around here for the week," she reviews. "You shouldn't have to do any more wash, or," she pauses, "just bring it to me when you drop him home. Don't do any cleaning. Have some vacation! Got that?"

Then, with a kiss and a hug, she slips into her car, belts herself in, gives the gas enough pressure to spurt her up the steep hill with a gravelly crunch as her jade, special edition, 2006 L.L. Bean Subaru disappears down the lane (the one she bought new when she was 80!).

Inside, Dad's snoring replaces the car engine's grind. He will wake up hungry. I will go from being the world's oldest spoilt kid, to his care-taker. This week will find me packing a picnic and him off to Wolf Lake for lunch. We will bundle ourselves and lawn chairs into town for the Tuesday evening concert. I'll follow his directions, leading us through the Nicolet National Forest backroads of his memories, reviving stories of hikes, hunting, and once getting lost. I will cook and he will say the prayers and thank me.

"Tempus fugit" — time flies, Dad often interjected. Time has changed our family dynamics, yet never changed our basic foundation of unconditional love. The future is as close as tomorrow. We can do this.

Don's last visit to the cabin, June 2013, sanding off leftover lumber scraps to make building blocks for his great-grandkids

Often heard in their conversations:

Regarding projects:

"That will happen... God willing and the creeks don't rise."

Regarding weather:

"Red sky in morning, sailors take warning.

Red sky at night... sailors delight."

Don and Phyllis enjoying their 60th anniversary swing, 2006

One More Lesson

Growing up, mothers teach or demonstrate many of the life lessons their daughters need to know. These might change over the generations, as with the lost art of ironing. I teased my mom for the lengths she went to after taking the clothes off the line with minimal wrinkles before taking out the ironing board, iron, and distilled water for steaming. There is a picture Dad took when I was about three with Mom beginning my gender-role education.

We are in the kitchen of their second parsonage, Mom with her hair wrap on, holding the curlers in place, and me on an elevated stool. I was placed at the narrow end of the ironing board with my toy iron and a handkerchief with Mom behind me, adult-sized iron and a sheet.

We were both smiling. I gave up ironing as soon as new materials were invented and permanent press erased that tradition for me – but not her.

I kidded her about her excesses in ironing (nearly) everything. In the 1960s, baggy sweatshirts and wrinkly T-shirts came into vogue. She was, in her word, horrified. She continued through that phase, ironing everything, including my work clothes. Now, I wish I could hug her and ask forgiveness for my insensitive remarks. It was a way to show her love and care for us as a family, not a mandate for me to continue. I realized the summer after she died that I was putting my head down for the last time on one of her ironed pillowcases. I wept.

Ironing was second to her sacred ritual of hanging up the clothes.

"Oh, the smell of fresh, air-dried laundry," she would purr with her nose stuck up into the folds of the current piece of wash she was removing from the line. Eyes closed in a blissful whiff, she'd gingerly fold the towels, sheets, blouses and haul them in the house... to her ironing board. She must have overlooked the replacement of that fresh air with steamed scents, but it was all part of the art of cleanliness — that being close to godliness, another desirable trait.

I enjoyed being outside, so putting up the laundry was a favorite way to be helpful. The main rule was to hang underpants on the inside lines, hidden by larger items on the outer edges, thus veiling "intimate" apparel from view. The rest was a mystery until that day at the cabin. One piece of clothing after another were obviously being placed precisely by some internal plan.

"Well, of course," she admonished me. "It is an art of color, organization of theme, visual sizing," she put her hand on her hip. She was 73-years-old when she got around to teaching me her system.

"Just hang things together, that are related in terms of use, size, and color. Put the largest things at the ends of the line and preferably, to the back. Hang the smaller things to the center. This keeps the line from sagging in the middle and helps to maintain a sort of balance — both in terms of weight and appearance. Put private things, like underwear, out of sight of the neighbors. The end result should be colorful and pleasant to the eye."

A one-dimensional look at this isn't enough. Maybe I'm overthinking, but I see life lessons in her need for balance, color, not letting the neighbors see the "dirty laundry" and organize things in a useful manner. She likely didn't think of this as her philosophy of life, but it's there.

The last thing she taught me about appearances was a month before she died. She was weak, but insisted on using the walker and dragging the oxygen tubing behind her to go to the bathroom mirror and apply her make-up. "I need to have my routine," she explained. "If I don't take care of myself..." her sentence hung between us, unspoken.

On that day, I held her steady, helping her lean into the sink, select a slender make-up brush and watched her touch it to the white, concealing powder in the compact. "Here," she directed. "I splurged on this special make-up to cover the darkness under my eyes. Just take a little powder and brush it under your eyes after putting on the foundation," she demonstrated. "Be sure you take this – an inheritance from me – because you've already inherited your dad's baggy eyes!"

Yes, I had, and I did. Thanks, Mom, for one last lesson.

Memories

Phyllis' art of hanging clothes

Phyllis always set an elegant table

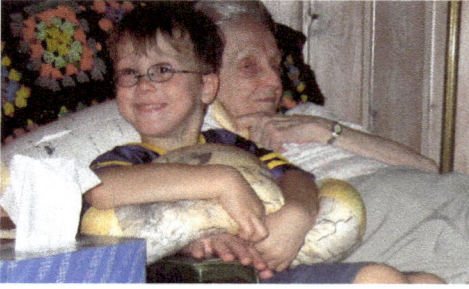

Phyllis snuggles with great-grandson James

Phyllis grabs an embrace from grandson Greg, who thought she was the best cook in the whole world

Phyllis gazing at her flower garden, which would be remembered as her legacy

Lois' thrift-shop shower invention, with Phyllis doing a demo

Steven, Phyllis, and Janet, early 1960s

Great-grandson James challenges Phyllis to a game of checkers as great-granddaughter Ella looks on

Fish Tails

"When the wind is in the west, the fish bite the best, but when the wind is in the east, the fish bite the least."

Dad Goes Fishing
Everything in its Own Good Time

*T*oday is his last chance. We've been at the cabin for two weeks and this is the first day of sunshine and a temperature over 70 degrees. The nights have dipped into the 40s with sporadic frost. This is neither spring nor fall, but June in Wisconsin. Today, the May flies are finally hatching. Dad, repeating his mantra, "I only live five minutes at a time," stood up from the breakfast table and catapulted himself way into the future by announcing, "Today, I'm going to go fishing!"

Mom and I exchanged glances across our bowls of oatmeal, having heard that before. It seemed something always got in his path and led him along until day's end. What would it be this time?

We cleared the table, heated the water, did the dishes, and put them in the rack to dry in the kitchen breeze. After our habitual walk with Jake, my 12-year-old pup and personal trainer, we went our separate ways. Mom picked up the baskets of dirty clothes, loaded them into the car, and headed to the laundry in town. I took my journal to the kayak with a plan to paddle against the waves and gradually float back. And yes, Dad was headed to the boat house. I so hoped he was serious about leaving his incessant puttsing to finally cast his line out to bring in supper.

Several hours later, I floated back into the cabin bay, noticing his boat tied to the dock, gently bobbing in the waves. Had he gone out and come back? If so, I hadn't seen him during my float. I peered

up the hill through the clearing to where the cabin sits on the ledge. Something didn't look quite right. I saw clothes fluttering in the wind, but they were sideways. I squinted into the sun and made out the form of my mother holding the clothesline over her head!

"What happened?" I yelled up the bank.

"The old cedar post caved in," Mom yelled back while trying to keep the sheets off the ground. "Your dad is getting some iron posts to prop it up!"

I quickly paddled to the dock, jumped out, and caught up to Dad as he wedged a recycled post into the ground. Standing back and brushing off his hands, he proudly reported, "If I hadn't walked past that post this morning and decided to pull it up, I wouldn't have been able to fix this."

I looked at the repair job. Two posts leaned in, wrapped with bungy cords and an old leather belt.

"What's with the belt?" I asked.

"Oh, that isn't for the post," he reassured me. "See the cut-out jug hanging there? It slips onto the belt. I wear it for berry picking!"

"And the post?" I reminded him.

"I had it over by the woodshed. I don't know how many times I have thought to move it, and this morning, when I passed it to fill the wood box, I did! It was stuck, so I had to rig a chain to loosen it. The chains are in the boathouse. Inside the door, I passed the worms, so I thought I'd take a minute and check them. Remember those dozen fat night crawlers I bought? Well, I mixed a batch of peat and water and stuck them all in that Magic Worm Ranch box last night. But, can you believe? They are all gone! Every last one of them! Must have been a slight space under the lid and they all got on each other's shoulders and climbed out! That was three whole dollars of prime worms, GONE! Those little ones just won't be as appetizing as the night crawlers! By this time, your mom was home with the laundry. I heard a yelp and there she was, holding up the lines to keep the clothes from going into the garden! Those cedar posts are something! They lasted 12 years."

It is now late afternoon. I sit in the shade of his new $5.00 umbrella. After the clothes pole incident, he had again wandered in the direction of the boathouse, only to pass the old metal table, left behind after a real estate sale. From his scrap wood, he scoured up a feasible board and spent a piece of afternoon carving a hole, where he would place the umbrella pole. He moved the new arrangement to the lakefront for the unveiling. By some miracle, as he opened the umbrella, its lime green and yellow stripes perfectly matched the table, previously painted from spray cans, left over from yet another project!

It will be evening before I look out on the lake and watch as he casts from his Starcraft between the fallen birch snags along the shore. This is how I had imagined it. Dad, dipping his fishnet under an arching rod. I am pleased to report that he will return with a stringer full of sunnies, rock bass, and bluegills. Tomorrow, he will pump water over the freshly cleaned catch before turning them over to Mom. She will fry them up and add a side salad. I will set the table on the porch and make fresh ice tea.

When we are all seated, he will slowly look at us and say: "Everything in its own good time. Yes, everything in its own good time."

Memories

Daddy Donald introduces daughter Janet to his catch, 1950s

Donald finally finishes puttsing & goes fishing

Donald brings home fish for lunch, 1980s

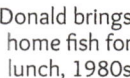

Greg and his cousin Jake, now a fishing guide in Alaska, 1980s

Cindy carrying on the tradition with James, 2020s

Greg and Ella catch another monster fish from under the dock, 2010s

Fish Bones

"*A*nd then, she died," my mother would often say, capping off her tales of misfortune or bad choices while insinuating somber warning and finalizing credence to her motherly advice.

On this occasion, she impressed upon us the relationship of serving bread with fish.

When Dad wasn't puttsing around the cabin, he was in his fishing boat. Several times a week, he'd bring in a stringer full of bluegills, perch, sunfish, and the occasional crappie. After a night in the live box chained to the dock, he'd carry his catch up to the pump and release them into an old cooler. There, at the edge of the rock wall, he'd fill two pans with water, one for washing away the scales and one for the cleaned fillets. Alongside the pans, he'd line up his collection of knives on his cleaning table, fashioned from a discarded kitchen counter top loosely nailed to a few two by fours.

I never did get the hang of piercing fish heads off while tails flapped in their unsuccessful attempt to escape to the ground. I expected this had to hurt and looked away. Dad, however, was already a trapper of gophers and muskrats before he hit puberty, so these deaths were part of life. He came from a generation that still gleaned much of their diets from the land. I respected that and knew if times on earth got bad, I wanted him to be at my side!

As good as he was at fish cleaning, he never mastered the talent of a boneless fillet as there were always little, almost invisible bones left in those fishy bodies. It was up to Mom to do the second round of quality control when she shook them in the brown paper bag of flour, salt, and paprika. Even with that, she would dish them onto our plate with the warning, "Now, watch out for any bones. There might still be some. Take a good look and chew slowly."

Then, she'd hand around the plate with the four slices of white bread, one for each of us. "Keep your bread handy," she counseled. It's a good idea to take a bite of bread after each bite of fish, just in case."

"Just in case what?" might be the question a guest at our table would ask. But my brother and I knew what was coming.

"You have to have a piece of bread when you eat fish, in case a bone goes down wrong." She would pause to let that life lesson sink in. "You could choke and die," she'd solemnly report.

"Once, a little boy got a bone stuck in his throat and they had to rush him to the hospital," she reminded us.

In this case, I knew the story to be true. My father, then a minister, was called away from our table more than once to attend to someone. We were eating supper the evening the phone call came in. Dad swiped his napkin off his lap, grabbed his coat, and was out the door — "That little Thompson kid swallowed a fish bone," he yelled over his shoulder. "I'm headed to the hospital."

My brother and I looked at each other, wide-eyed. This little boy just could not die. He was too close to our ages. We looked back down at our plates grateful we were not having fish for supper. Mom looked over at us with her "all-knowing" nod.

It would be hours before the garage door opened and we all hustled to the kitchen entry holding our breath. Would Mom's "and, then he died," be the ending to yet another story?

Dad's face didn't reveal a clue. He rounded us up back at the supper table and motioned for us to sit.

"The bone went down the boy's throat, making a cut as it went," he began. "They had to do a minor surgery to dislodge it. They used local anesthesia, so it had to be scary for that kiddo." Dad bobbed his head, emphasizing every detail.

"Did he die?" my brother and I blurted out together. Mom leaned in.

"No, but he'll be in the hospital overnight for observation. It surely gave us a fright though."

That was enough for my brother and I to spend the rest of our lives serving bread with fish and chewing carefully. We didn't want our fish story to end with, "and then... they died!"

Sucker Babies

*B*ugs, butterflies, clams, snails, rocks, tropical fish, let me tell you about my brother, Steven. From earliest times, that boy was curious, collecting things, putting them in boxes with compartments or pinning wings into display cases. He memorized their names, looked up their life stories and, by age 14, was working (with special permission as an underaged minor) at Michelle's, the neighborhood pet shop.

At the cabin, Steven spent hours belly down, on the dock or inside the green rowboat, scouring the bottom of the lake with his roaming eyes watching underwater plants, fish eggs, and iridescent slime. In season, he used a little scoop net to catch tadpoles, checking for their progress toward frog-dom. He was fascinated with minnows, water bugs, marshland pitcher-plants, and dragonflies. In the spring, we'd find the husks they left behind on the cabin walls and lakeside rocks, little, empty containers where googley eyes and iridescent wings formed.

That brings us to the day at the cabin when Steven had an idea.

The suckers were running. First, one must know that suckers are fish, a bottom feeding sort of creature with, well... suckers for mouths. Each spring, they swim up the creek, much like I suppose salmon do. I've never seen them in the lake, but each spring, they show up to spawn by the bridge. Dad used to fish for them and smoke them in an old refrigerator — however that worked. On this day, we were coming back from town and stopped at the bridge to see if the sucker run had begun.

It had! The water was foaming with splashing fish, all trying to jump over each other to get to the pond beyond the downed log. Dad pulled his fish net out of the trunk and made some passes through the bubbling frenzy, pulling out three large fish. He brought them up to the bank, where Steve and I waited for a closer look.

"See this one?" Dad pointed to a fish with an elongated belly. "She is full of eggs." he explained before rubbing his thumb down the length of the fish. Steve and I sat spellbound, as a gooey liquid oozed to the ground.

Then, in a perfect use of an opportunity, Dad picked up the other one, expressing a milky substance, explaining that it was sperm. I don't remember our ages, but we hadn't been given the "talk" about birds and bees, at least not with such visuals.

With that, Steven perked up and asked, "Dad, do you have a jar in the car? Something we could collect this in?" he ended, producing a disturbing grimace from our mother.

A quick look in the trunk yielded a receptacle that would do. "I would like to collect some of these eggs and cover them with that sperm," Steven explained. "Maybe I can hatch some baby suckers!"

In the spirit of science and being a supportive parent, my father put his net back in the water and soon produced a few more specimens. Stever had no hesitations in picking them up and following Dad's example, milking both eggs and sperm into his container for his experiment. Finally, he filled the rest of the jar with creek water, fixed on the lid and put his treasure into the trunk. Up the hill we went, back to the cabin for lunch and an afternoon of swimming.

Days passed. Maybe a week. The sucker run was over and so was our memory of the jar filled with eggs and sperm. That is, until the next time we went to town. Oh, what a stench! What could it possibly be? It didn't come from the front seat. Nothing in the back seat. But, oh what a cloud of unspeakable aromas escaped into the air when the trunk was opened!

All of our noses crinkled. Mom looked at Dad. Dad looked at Steven. I retreated out of sight. I think it was Dad who gingerly removed the offending container from the trunk and walked it to the creek, where the fermented brew was released into the current.

It wasn't caviar and it wasn't viable for sucker incubation. It was a foreshadowing of Steve's future life, traveling to the Caribbean on buying trips for Chicago's Old Town Aquarium, choosing tropical fish for propagation in their 100-gallon fish tanks.

Steven also used those 100-gallon tanks for Boa Constrictors that required live rats for food. His real talent was as a musician. He became a professional oboe player, including orchestras in Florida – an especially proud moment for us was when he played a solo with the Chicago Symphony Orchestra. As all starving artists, he kept his day job. With that, Steven had a talking parrot, baby-sat Boas, and successfully raised, among others, Angel Fish and Blue Bettas, brought back from his tropical "fishing" trips.

With Our Bare Hands

Previously published in
Lake Country Journal May/June 2000

*H*e was six years old that summer at the lake. Sun-sparkled waves lapped around the weatherworn plank pier where he would lie on his stomach and peek into the old fishbox. Grandpa would often stop his chores, hand Gregory a spade and an empty soup can, and send him to the decaying leaf pile by the boathouse to dig for nightcrawlers.

There were still a few cane poles leaning in the shed, with lines, hooks, sinkers, and red-and-white bobbers attached. The paint-chipped, green, wooden rowboat, with a cement-filled ham-can anchor, was moored along my father's handcrafted pier.

But that day my son Gregory and I were alone. We had taken our sandwiches and juice down for a picnic on the dock. I could feel the occasional nail head popping up through the graying boards, barely covered by faded redwood stain. We laid down a beach towel to protect ourselves from slivers.

Our bellies full, we stretched out. Looking up at the clouds and identifying their shapes was a favorite game. When they floated into sight, we'd ask each other, "What do you think that one is?" Or, "Did you see that dragon?" That day, Gregory saw something special.

"Look, Mom," he yelled, "An eagle! A real one!" We never got tired of eagles. Or loons. Or blue herons.

Instead of gliding down the length of the lake and disappearing, this eagle circled the cove across from us. It folded its wings and swooped down into the waves, baring its claws. But on the upswing, they remained empty.

"Must have missed the fish," I mused aloud. We were about to return to our cloud gazing when the eagle circled again. Again, the dive, the pause in the water, the empty talons. This was repeated several times.

"There must be something pretty big over there for an eagle to be losing the battle," I suggested. Again, the eagle missed. "I gotta know what is going on. What do you say, Greg? Shall we go over and take a look?"

I felt the need to hurry. What if we didn't get there in time to see what it was? It could get away. Or, the eagle would finally get it, but – wait, maybe it should be saved. After all, it had put up a good fight. Didn't it deserve to live?

The green rowboat was ready to go. "Jump in, get that orange life preserver tied up tight. Sit in the front and guide me," I spat out the orders. Rowing was not as fast as a motorboat, but it offered a quieter, sneak approach.

"Pull on the right – harder!" Greg ordered.

The waves were against us. The breeze added to the work. "Straight – both oars – harder!" Greg's directions matched my urgency.

We passed Grass Island, the huge shallow weed bed, and went into a float about 20 feet from the last dive landing. The eagle wasn't fooled by our casual pose. On the next circle, he rode an air current up into a tall white pine and lit on a branch.

"Will that eagle dive-bomb us if we go over there?" Greg asked.

"We'll hope he's not that hungry." I didn't know what an eagle was capable of in attack mode. Greg looked like a Viking masthead stretched out over the point of the green rowboat as he surveyed the cove. "What do you see?" I asked him.

"By the shore – something white. It's a big... it's a really big... fish! It looks dead – belly up. It's rocking with the waves," he finished.

I pulled the right oar and then the left, before sinking them into the water to slow us from a direct hit.

"Mom, do you think it's alive? Look at those teeth! Do we dare touch it? Oh, Mom, can we take it home?"

After inspecting it with the end of the oar, I pronounced it dead. The eagle watched us from his branch. Should we call this a mystery solved or go with Gregory's suggestion? After a trip to the taxidermist, it would make a dandy surprise gift for Dad.

I'd heard fish stories all my life, but rarely saw anything bigger than a snapping turtle or stringers full of panfish. After each fish tale, with arms spread wide to indicate the length of the latest muskie, no one ever told where it had been caught. This fish on a wall would make the greatest trophy.

"Greg," I asked, "Do you think we can get this baby into the boat?" We hadn't brought a net, since we had no intention of capturing the eagle's prey. "If we both lean over the same side of the boat to pull this guy in, we'll end up in the lake with him!" I scanned the contents of the boat.

"You sit as far as you can to that side and I'll try to pull him up over the edge. Put the anchor over by you."

I put my arms into the water – nothing – the waves rocked him out of my grasp. I grabbed again and felt slimy fins and his slippery tail, but the other end has a gaping mouth with all its sharp teeth. Again, I repositioned myself, and, like the eagle, I missed.

I don't remember which one of us saw it first, but inside the boat was a length of rope. I hauled my upper body back into the boat, made a noose and, after several tries, Greg yelled, "You got it, Mom! Pull tight!"

I crawled back into the middle seat and adjusted myself for rowing. Gregory edged the muskie to the back of the boat and prepared to tow. The rope jerked and tightened around its tail. It held and off we went, the eagle following our departure.

Back at the dock, we were stuck again. The fish floated fine while being towed, but how would we get it out of the lake? I hated the idea of hugging it around the neck while Greg pulled the tail rope. I left him holding on while I retrieved one of Dad's larger fishing nets. On the count of three, I scooped and Gregory tugged. First a plop and then a thud. The muskie was landed — head to tail, across the width of the dock.

Now, how would we get this monster up the hill? Into the car? Off to town?

"Greg, I'm going up to the cabin. I want to take a few pictures and then look for a box. I think, if we get it inside, we won't hurt it. I don't want to drag it and lose more scales. Look where the eagle claws went in," I said, pointing out some damage.

Gregory sat with our little Loch Ness monster until I returned, armed with a camera, a yardstick, and a box. Neither of us could hold it up for a photo. We couldn't budge it off the ground.

We maneuvered the fish into the box. In order to ascend the dozen or so earthen steps to the cabin, we had to lift at the same time to clear just one. By taking turns pushing and pulling, we slid the box to the top and next to the car.

"Oh, Greg! This is going to be great — walking down the streets of Three Lakes in the middle of the afternoon with the biggest darn fish they've seen in a long time!"

The parking spot in front of Jerry's Bait was taken, so we moved into the next closest — right in front of the American Legion Bar. The door was open and a few patrons were standing around the counter inside.

I popped open the trunk. Gregory stood beside me. It would be hard on our backs to go for a direct lift. Somehow, we scooted it over and onto the curb, where we took a moment to catch our breath. That was all it took. One, two, three guys came out of the bar, glasses in hand.

"Whoa, that is a big fish, little lady!" one exclaimed.

"Yes, it is," I calmly replied, giving Gregory a don't-you-dare-say-a-word look.

"Did you catch that yourself?" a second man queried.

"Actually, no. My son here helped me pull it in."

"Were you fishing one of these lakes around town?" asked the third.

"No, we're on a lake just a bit north," I hedged. Darned if I was going to tell them!

We started pushing and pulling our muskie's box towards Jerry's Bait Shop.

"How big is that muskie, do you know?" ask another man who had just joined us.

"We're headed to Jerry's to get an official read — we wouldn't want to be telling any tall tales," I grinned at him and winked at Greg.

And finally, the question I was waiting for: "So, what did you use to catch that beauty?"

I stopped pushing. Gregory stopped pulling. We both stretched up to our tallest height.

"What did we use to catch this beauty?" I paused, making eye contact with each and every one of them. "How did we catch this prize, you want to know?"

I inhaled deeply and exhaled my answer slowly:

"We... caught... it... with... our... bare... hands."

At Jerry's, the crowd watched as the muskie was weighed and measured out front by the display case. It measured 44 inches – nearly Greg's height and a mere 16 inches shorter than me – weighing in at 21 pounds.

We took it to Bonack's Taxidermy. Unfortunately, our muskie had been dead a few days, making a wall hanging impossible. An autopsy declared "two good-sized suckers stuck in the muskie's throat was the cause of death." I regret that I did not at least claim the head for the collection Dad kept on the inside of the boathouse door. We do not know what became of the muskie – although we never checked back at the Legion nor Jerry's to see if it was hanging on a wall.

Greg measuring his Muskie, caught with his bare hands

Memories

Grandpa Don takes his grandson fishing through the years (1979-1997)
One of Greg's favorite memories

Row, Row, Row Your Boat...
Life is But a Dream

Boy in a Rowboat
(Steve at 10)

Skinny boy perched out over the bow of a green,
   paint-chipped, wooden rowboat,
the mast-head of his own sailing vessel.

His oars taste the tips of waves,
sparkling their way into the east inlet bay,
chock full of purple pickerelweeds and lily flowers.

Lilies whose pads begin to show their varicose veins
and rust age spots in the lateness of summer,
succumb to months of soaking in the sun.

On one knee, he balances, head stretched over the waters,
below, among the seaweed, shiner minnows,
glint with each twitch of their tails.

A pointer pup, he patiently hunts the frogs of August,
once-upon-a-time wiggly tadpoles of June. Poised stoically,
another hunter, the statuesque Great Blue Heron tiptoes
through the shoreline reeds, stealthily stalking
those very frogs from among the grassy bogs.

From the sky, an eagle's shadow swoops down to touch him,
As he and his childhood float lazily by.

Creepy Kayaks

The kayaks were laid out along the bank by the short dock in front of the boathouse. There were two orange, open faced kayaks for the girls, a longer open kayak for Lois, and my Blue Breeze, the longest at 18 feet and the only enclosed vessel. It included adjustable leg brackets and an internal inflatable triangular innertube, evidently needed to keep me afloat. After swimming, we planned to kayak east to a cove we call the Pot Hole, where beavers and frogs reside.

"OK, kids," I yelled out, "time to get out of the water and put on your life preservers. I'll meet you on the bank."

Ella reached hers first and let out a long, "Eeuu! My kayak is crawling with ants! What am I going to do?"

"What can you do?" I asked back, practicing my critical thinking approach.

She started hopping around the perimeter, hands flapping in the air. "Ohhhh," she shuddered, "There are spiders, too!"

By now, Avery was peering at her kayak's inhabitants, shoulders quivering, but not a sound.

I spotted a daddy long-legs coming off of a reed bent over the boat. I picked him up and held it for the girls to see.

"Ella," I asked, "Didn't I tell you about the daddy long-legs? You hold him like this and ask him, 'Where are my cows?' One leg will point straight out and that is where you'll find them!"

It occurred to me that this meant precious little to a generation of kids that don't have cows and, furthermore, by merely turning in a circle, those cows could be anywhere in a 360° radius. However, in the moment, fear is replaced by curiosity. Both girls moved in closer for the demonstration, but did not participate.

I did decide to participate in the preview of my kayak with its dark cavern, just in case. I declared it good to go and we shoved off, gliding over lily pads and into the waves.

We had barely been on the water for five minutes when I heard Ella let out a screech followed, this time, by Avery. They had entwined their kayaks to form a raft and were splashing their paddles into a froth. I headed their direction, not so much concerned about them being dumped into the lake as the tenor of their screaming.

"Girls," I called out, pulling up next to them, "Is there a problem?"

"Spiders! Big spiders!" Ella trembled again. "You have to get them out of here! I can't do it!"

Avery was hunched down in her kayak, with the paddle poised in a defensive, yet useless, position.

"OK, everybody," I said, "Take a deep breath. We have to practice being calm. Know that you aren't in any danger even if you fall out of the kayak. It will not sink and you have your preservers on plus your whistles, if you really need help." They both nodded and inhaled slowly.

I edged to Ella's side, leaned over and took another daddy long-legs off her kayak. "Remember, he is a friendly spider. He will not bite. He'll just help you find your cows," I laughed and continued, "Isn't it great we don't have any poisonous critters around here?"

They both meekly nodded in agreement, adjusted themselves into the center of their kayaks, and followed Lois around the bend.

Before I had time to rearrange my butt in the seat, I felt something wiggle, no slither, over my foot. I knew, without looking, what was riding along with me. It happened last week, too. There wasn't a milli-second between the slither and my scream. "Oh my god, no! Not another one!"

I swung my behind up on the back of the kayak, flailing my legs to either side of the kayak's opening and balanced before the kayak jerked sideways. Then, I looked down. There, on the floor, a long garter snake curled his way from under my seat to the spot under the inflatable triangle and disappeared.

The girls shoved their paddles into a stop. "What is it, Nana?" Ella yelled over the waves.

"A SNAKE!" I yelled back, hoping there was only one, not two, like last week.

All my brave words about spiders evaporated in the face of this snake. Did this irrational fear date back to Eve in the Garden? What was I going to do?

Lois was now paddling toward me. I eased myself into a balanced position and paddled to shore, jumped into the water, and stared back into the cavity of my kayak.

Yup, there it was. Maybe if I pulled the inflatable out, I could see it better. I grabbed the red air tube to remove it, just as Lois drew up alongside and let go an audible gasp.

"Oh, oh," she said breathlessly, "I thought that red tube was your snake!"

This time, I was able to laugh. "No, my snake is in here," I pointed. Why can't I bring myself to just reach in, grab him and... I tried to reason that he was just a measly, frightened, albeit creepy, garter snake.

Lois broke into my thoughts. "Jan, can you tilt the kayak toward me? I'll pick him up and give him a good toss."

And, she did. The girls pulled up just in time to see him fly over my head and eagerly swim away.

I pulled out the inflatable, checked under my seat, pounded on the sides, replaced everything, and gingerly slid myself back into the kayak. My cellular memory could still feel him slithering over my foot. What had I said earlier about breathing slowly?

Sheepishly, I glanced over to the girls.

"Oh, kids, I can't believe that I gave you some pointers about how to stay calm on the water and get over those spiders, only to lose it over a snake!"

"Oh, Lois," I added, "So much for being a role model!"

As the girls pointed their kayaks back toward the Pot Hole, I called out my last advice:

"Do as I say, not as I do," just to make sure all was not lost on today's lesson.

Ella and Lilly waiting for Lois and Jan to hurry up so they can all go kayaking

Avery and Ella preparing to inner tube with their flippers

The Inner Tube

The inner tube ritual happens after 3:00 p.m. — my mom's declared "sun time" for being more protected from direct, cancer-causing rays. A slathering of sunscreen is applied, followed by an additional T-shirt to shelter my shoulders and back. I adjust my sunhat, tightening it under my chin, and put on sunglasses for the glare. Finally, I hoist the inner tube into the water, sit at the dock steps, and struggle into my flippers like Cinderella's step-sisters squeezing into her glass slippers. I fit myself into the tube's center.

It is a lovely way to ease into the water and allows some time to get used to the temperature. It also gets ones' feet off the bottom, if clams and rocks are a concern. Or, maybe a leech. Or, slimy seaweed slithering around your legs. Or, or, or... a snapping turtle under the dock?

There sure are some big ones that lay their eggs down by the creek. I remember going to the bridge and seeing them plant their treasures into a hole, blocking the road. Dad used to get out of the car, find a large stick and poke its nose until it took a bite, allowing Dad to pick it up and remove it to the side of the lane.

My mind races back to Grandpa Zager catching them and giving them to his wife, Alma, for turtle soup. And, there is that picture of my dad holding one up by its tail, the shell as large as a bushel basket. Remember when...

I pull my thoughts back to the warmth of the water and the waves gently rocking me along the shoreline. I don't have goggles, but like to stare down into the water from my front position. My arms hang over the tube, doing a sort of breast-stroke while I gaze into the depths. I can see my flippers dangling below me, swishing the weeds back and forth. The lake is mostly clear with a root beer tinge to it. The rust color identifies local boats with their side streaks. My T-shirt has taken on the hue. Maybe even my hair.

It's getting shallow now. My flippers touch bottom and scare up a school of minnows. A longer-fish swishes below me. Could it be a northern? I'm used to hearing about muskies in the lake. Greg was about six years old when we saw that eagle circling and pulled out that muskie "with our bare hands" – I'm just saying. Muskies have teeth. Do they bite swimmers? Once I read about a 12-year-old boy that was bitten in the leg while swimming, in a lake, not too far from here! I look down at my legs and make a few rapid jutting splashes. I flip around and put my legs over the tube's rim and begin a sort of backstroke, only to note that now my butt is hanging down the tube's center hole, exposed to possible chomping.

Sure am glad we don't have any alligators and crocodies here. But wait. What about those crazy people in Florida that want exotic snakes for pets and then just let them go in the Everglades? What if they bring their little pet alligators with them on vacation and decide to throw them in the lake when they get bored with them?

I look over the edge of my tube, just to check. I know better, but am now on a roll. Certainly, I reason, no alligator could survive more than a few weeks here. Other than that big inflatable alligator I saw at the Fleazaar fundraiser. It would be a good joke to let it float about the lake, but the long-term effect on people would not be funny. Why am I thinking about this, anyway?

I take these expeditions to cool off, to get some exercise, to see the shoreline go by at the slowest speed possible on the lake. I listen to fish smacking the water. I see the individual leaves and pinecones on the trees. I watch the kingfishers dive. I close my eyes to the sun and see sparkles on the insides of my eyelids. I dream of being submerged in this water, gliding along as I am today, when I am far away. When it is January. When I'm on an airplane taking off. When I need to breathe.

A tickle on my leg brings me back to reality. A dragonfly with its big roaming eyes and iridescent wings lands to hitch a ride. I am pleased to give her a lift, as we both dry off our legs in the sun, drifting with the waves, to the end of the lake, on my big, tractor-tire inner tube.

Phyllis continued to inner tube with her flippers until her last visit in 2018, aged 92

On a Summer's Day

I take a stroke and move my kayak over the mirrored lake.
I glide.

I raise my face to the sun, eyes closed.
I sigh.

I dip my toes into the splashing waves.
I grin.

I float over reflected clouds, kaleidoscoped by wind on waves.
They shimmer.

I release myself to peace,
On a Summer's Day.

Ella's haiku from Girls' Camp 2024

We have had some fun
Two women out in the woods
Some work and some play

Paddling Songs

The Voyageurs had songs to paddle by and so did we. The following are a few examples:

The Ants
The ants went marching one by one,
Hurrah, hurrah,
The ants went marching one by one,
Hurrah, hurrah,
The ants went marching one by one,
The little one stopped to suck his thumb.
And they all went marching,
Down, to the earth, to get out of the rain,
Boom, boom, boom...

(Two by two, the little one stopped to tie his shoe;
Three by three, the little one stopped to climb a tree;
Four by four, the little one stopped to shut the door;
Five by five, the little one stopped to look in a hive;
Six by six, the little one stopped to pick up some sticks;
Seven by seven, the little one thought he'd gone to heaven;
Eight by eight, the little one stopped to open the gate;
Nine by nine, the little one stopped to pick up a dime;
Ten by ten, the little one stopped to say: THE END)

Row, Row, Row your boat became:

Propel, propel, propel your craft,
Placidly down the liquid solution,
Merrily, merrily, merrily, merrily,
Life is but an illusion.

Noah

Oh, the Lord said to Noah, there's going to be a floody, floody,
The Lord said to Noah, there's going to be a floody, floody,
GET MY PEOPLE,
(Slap paddle on the water – Splash!)
out of the muddy, muddy,
Children of the Lord.

Oh, the Lord said to Noah, you've got to build and arkie, arkie,
The Lord said to Noah, you've got to build an arkie, arkie,
Build it out of (slap paddle on the water – Splash!) birchie barkie,
barkie
Children of the Lord.

The Other Day, I saw a Bear

This is a call and response with every line being repeated by a second singer, group, or echoed.

1) The other day (repeat),
   I saw a bear (repeat)
   A great big bear (repeat)
   Just standing there. (repeat)
   (sing all the way through without repeating)

2) He looked at me (2x)
   I looked at him (2x)
   He sized up me (2x)
   I sized up him. (2x)
   (repeat)

3) He said to me,
   You better run,
   For I see you ain't
   Got any gun.
   (repeat)

4) And so I ran,
   Away from there
   And right behind
   me came that bear.
   (repeat)

5) And up ahead
   I saw a tree
   A great big tree
   Oh glory be!
   (repeat)

6) And so I jumped
   Into the air
   But I missed that branch
   Away up there.
   (repeat)

7) Now don't you fret
   And don't you frown
   For I caught that branch
   On the way back down.
   (repeat)

8) And that's the end
   There ain't no more
   Unless I see
   That bear once more.
   AND THAT'S THE END
   THERE AIN'T NO MORE
   Unless I see that
   Bear once more!

This was sung while paddling down the creek as teens — one of many camp songs — and later when Baby James got up in the middle of the night and needed to be sung back to sleep. I also sang LA LLORONA in Spanish to him, because I knew all of the verses, but it is a lament. No problem, I guess. He didn't understand Spanish anyway!

Memories

Phyllis, in her floating lawn chair, and Janet in her inner tube

Janet gives Phyllis a ride in her Tia-juana taxi

Phyllis and Janet, 1953

Janet with son Greg, 1979

A flotilla of friends and family

The Three Bears

Auntie Wilma Gets Her Bear

When the town folks talked about my Auntie Wilma, they referred to her as the "old maid" school teacher. As a child, I understood that to mean she was not married and had one of the only jobs allowed to a woman in her unwed state. Through my father, I gleaned some stories of his 18-year-old sister being in charge of a one-room school housing five-year-old first graders through eighth graders, often including farm boys her same age. These older lads were annually required to help with the farm harvests, thus

prolonging the time it took to graduate. Wilma's job included arriving early to pump the water and stoke the stove. There are photos of her in front of various buildings surrounded by her brood.

I was too young to be fascinated with her stories, only realizing later the impact of living the "Old Maid" life label, when really being an example of women's rights. My dad recalled her first Model-T, her travel adventures to California and Mexico, and the rumor that she smoked. He was 13 years her junior, so his recollections came through a lens of still being a child himself. But, on that day at the cabin, they were both adults and I was old enough to comprehend the exchange!

Auntie Wilma Gets Her Bear

Auntie Wilma was one of the relatives who ventured out of northern Illinois villages and family farms to journey the freeway for hours before arriving at our two-tire-track-with-the-grass-in-the-middle lane ending at the lake. Once there, family members brought their woodstove cooking skills, fishing poles, and always took a motor boat ride around the lake. Auntie added one more attribute — she encouraged us, with money, to be creative.

Our creations were made with a few pine cones, some loose birch bark, a clam shell, and sprigs of ferns stuck together with Elmer's glue and pine pitch. She called these creations souvenirs, which we then put up for sale. Sale, that is, along the trail between our cabin and the neighbor on the Point. The half mile stretch connected the families on daily visits. When Auntie and Mom were leaving the cabin to hike to the next cabin, my brother, Steven, and I would gather our box of woodland crafts, ran ahead, and set up shop. Mothers are gracious and complimentary, but Aunt Wilma bought stuff! We saved her quarters for comic books, but I suspect all of those ferns glued to birch bark were readily recycled back to the woods.

On one particular summer our attention went from money-making to bear stories. Auntie arrived during a flurry of sightings. There was the bear that swam across the lake after being chased away by workers at the Point. There was the bear that slid down a tree in front of our car one night when returning from the dump, where the entertainment included tourists foolishly getting out of cars to feed all manner of creatures. Not us! My father sternly ingrained safety measures and warned of dangers. He was taking no chances.

Other than the dump, bears didn't show up on demand. Or did they? After a few days stay, Wilma had not witnessed any of the bears represented in the evening story-telling. No bear peered into the window where you could even "feel its hot breath" through the screens. No swimming bears. Not even signs of scat along the lare. Maybe Auntie got impatient with the no-shows. A few days before she left, she took matters into her own hands.

It was dusk, time for us younger ones to quit playing board games, brush teeth, and go to bed. It had become a ritual to look out all the windows, just in case there might be a racoon, a pack of coyotes howling, or, yes, a bear. All was quiet, but where was Wilma? Unbeknownst to anyone, she was outside by the woodpile, secretly placing slices of bacon among the sticks of firewood. From the dining area window, she would have a clear view of any action, a mere 20 feet away.

Sometime in the night, it happened. A bear picked up the scent of that bacon, came down the hill, stood up on his haunches and began picking off the strips of fat and making them his.

That would have been enough to satisfy Auntie's excitement, but it's what happened next that we remember.

After reaching one of the higher placed bacon strips, the bear came thudding back down to all fours. His paws touched off an avalanche of fire wood, cascading over the east bank toward the bay. At least that was the story told at breakfast the next morning.

What I did witness through the dining window was my father, one hand on hip and the other stretched out full length, with his pointer finger waving in the air. I could not hear what he was saying, but imagine it wasn't for young ears to hear. I could see Auntie's head bob into sight and then disappear again, just as another piece of firewood came flying back up the bank and onto the wood pile. One after another, the missiles flew over the edge, landing at my father's feet.

This time, the "Old Maid" school teacher was not in charge. She was on the receiving end. My father's message about bear etiquette was playing out in real time as my brother and I watched through the window. This was a prime example of natural consequences in the flesh. Steve and I were just glad it was Auntie's flesh and not our own! This incident did not detour our Auntie Wilma from returning to our woods, intent on finding more bear! She did, however, stop baiting with bacon.

Wilma and Donald having a better day

Guest book August 5, 1962

"The THRILLER day of all days!! There is no doubt about the bear -- A BIG BLACK BEAR! My first ever in Wisconsin!"
- Wilma Kurtz

Kathy and the Relay Race

*M*om was the middle child, Beulah being her older sister by five years, and Keith, barely a year younger, the male who would carry their last name, Wise, into the future. Keith later named his Charolais cattle farm and his real estate business – Wise Acres, as well as giving his last name to his three children, Linda, Kathy, and Kim. Kathy and Mom commiserated over their position in life as "the middle" child.

It was the summer of 1957 when Keith decided to bring his wife, Rachel, and the kids "up" to the cabin on Lake Julia. The cabin had only been carved out of the side of the esker that year, with construction done slowly during each visit with whatever lumber or sales items were available. At least the interior rooms had walls, allowing the family some privacy during visits.

In 1957, all of "us cousins" were under the age of ten. It was their first, and ended up being their only, visit to the cabin. No, I don't think it was a result of what happened, but life in Illinois got busy and too far away for a return. Kathy said it had nothing to do with the blood-sucking leech that fastened itself to her leg, nothing to do with big black spiders in the outhouse, and nothing to do with the bear.

1957 became known as: The Year of the Bear. Bear stories melded after numerous encounters, so exact dates ran amuck, but the who and where stuck clearly – facts to the storyteller and any onsite witnesses. The bear stories were told with relish, each listener ingesting details and some fear. In this story, Kathy is the literal pivot point. It was not a cold and rainy night, it was July 1, 1959, at the Kurtz cabin. (Guest book records!)

We cousins were immersed in many cabin activities. If it was 68 degrees, we were allowed to swim in the lake. If we had life preservers on, we could go out in the boat. If we were with an adult, we could hike to the creek to check on the minnow traps. If it was raining, we had inside games and toys. On this day, I guess we were sent outside to play while the women finished preparing supper. We were to stay close by so we could come quickly when called. Mom admonished us to respect the cooks by appearing while the food was still hot! Out the door we went.

The cabin's source of water, a creaky hand-pump, sits a few giant steps from the back door.

Someone came up with the idea to have a relay race from the pump, up the hill to a waiting player, run around them, come tearing back down the hill and touch the next runner. I don't recall teams nor timed competition. Likely, it was a parent's plan to have us run off extra energy.

We did a few trial runs, each practicing being the pivot point, sitting in the grass near the top of the steep hill. This hill has an angle that produced angst in drivers before the dawn of four-wheel drives. If it rained, repeated runs to make it to the top were frequent. Wet grass made these charges dangerous, sending cars sideways, tires spinning, and a retreat back to the pump required to save the tracks from turning into mud slides. We, however, were young children ages 2-9, eager to test our leg muscles and lungs. Lungs used to cheer each other on and, later, for screaming.

Next, it was Kathy's turn to sit up on the hill. While she walked into position, we arranged ourselves in order behind the starting line. "On your marks, get set, go," she yelled from her spot up the hill.

Off went Kim, up to his sister, touched her shoulder, circled around behind and back down. "Go, Kim, go!" we hollered. Down he came and touched Steven, next in line. Up he went, huffing and puffing, around Kathy, touch, back down, my brother reaching out to tap me next.

I watched closely as he came stumbling toward me on his two-year-old legs. "Go Steven!" we shouted, clapping our hands. I looked back up at Kathy and stopped.

On the cusp of the hill, some brush was moving. There wasn't any wind. Then, a black furry leg appeared out of the bush, then another and then, yes! An entire black bear's head! Yikes! He was easing himself diagonally across the hill toward the lake side, just yards behind where Kathy sat oblivious.

"A BEAR!" I yelled as Steven came across the finish. He skidded to a stop and looked where I was pointing. After a week of bear stories, I might just as well of yelled, "WOLF" while the whole village turned away.

"Really, Kathy! A bear behind you!" I screamed. By now, Kim and Steven saw it, too. We waved our hands, but she stayed put.

According to Kathy, she didn't believe us until we all took off running for the back door. "Bear!" I yelled as I passed the kitchen window. I got to the screen door, pulled it open, stepped out of the way and, to my surprise, the first one through the door, was... Kathy!

Reflection: At a reunion in 2022, we cousins had foggy memories of the men going out and looking over the hill toward the lake for the bear. Other than our witness, it was not seen. Kathy's eyes went wide as she repeated her story of the run down the hill, thus adding to our family cabin stories while my grandchildren listened on – the emotion of the moment still vivid. It was good to have our memories corroborated for the next generation's retelling!

The Wise cousins - Kathy and Linda in the back, Kim in front with Janet and Steven, 1957

James and the Whistle

James' eyes darted around the room, his curious three-year-old mind taking in his expanding world. I thought I had child proofed the place, but there he was, looking up at the whistle I had hung from the highest peg, out of his range, but obviously not out of sight.

"Nana, can you get that down?" he asked, pointing straight up at the big referee whistle.

"James, I only bring that down when I am going to take a walk in the woods. I put it around my neck to use if I get lost or if I see a bear," I explained, hoping that would satisfy him.

"Can I see it?" He asked again, using his best selective listening.

"If I get it down, I know you will want to blow it. Maybe if you touch it, make a little toot, just to hear how it sounds, and then we'll put it back up so we know where to find it when we go on a walk," I offered, thinking I'd been very generous. "Will that work?" I asked him, wondering why I thought that would end it!

He had hooked me in, but I wouldn't give it up without one more caution. "We'll try it quietly, because we're not going to get lost in the cabin and we surely don't want to find any bears in here. Now, go find Grandpa to help get it down."

Soon, James was back, instructing Grandpa to reach up and get him the whistle. Once in his eager hands, the whistle went right to his lips. James is not timid. The whistle let out a blast that rang through the cabin.

"James, we're inside!" I grimaced. "Just make little whistle sounds. Blow carefully. Little puffs, like this," I took a small breath and demonstrated.

The next five minutes were filled with a variety of tempos and decibels, mostly tolerable.

"Ok, James, time is up," I said. He dutifully held out the rope with the whistle and handed it toward me, then stopped. If a three-year-old boy ponders, that is what he did next.

He tipped his head to one side, looked at the whistle and then back at me. "Nana," he took a deep, pensive breath, "Nana, I think we should go on a walk. We can go out in the woods, find a bear, and then... whistle!"

Donald always challenged us to find the 16 bears in this photo, and after years, we decided there were only 15. Hm... Was this his idea of a joke?

Also Donald's handwritten note with another cabin rule of how to pump water. Don't be a jerk!

James at Four

James Has Something to Say

Four-year-old James and I were on the dock, obediently watching his eight-year-old sister, Ella, perform antics in the waters of Lake Julia. At the moment, she was being a mermaid under the July afternoon sun, collecting lily pads and seaweed for her food.

"Watch me, watch me!" she commanded before dipping below the waves, scattering the pan fish waiting for bread crumbs under the dock.

As commanded, we watched her disappear below the surface, coming up momentarily, sputtering, clutching a clam in her hand. "Look at this," she directed us before asking, "Do mermaids eat these?"

"I don't know, Ella," I confessed. "I guess I always thought of mermaids as vegetarians, being related to fish and all. But a clam? Maybe." She tossed it back into the shallows where it sunk slowly to the sand.

James watched its descent intently, the moving waters cradling it to a soft landing. He paused and looked over to the spot where reeds met the yellow lily flowers, the spot I pointed out when telling him a story of his great-great-grandpa Ford the day before.

In a tone beyond his years, James declared, "I have something to say." In unquestionable seriousness, he continued. "When I was older," he paused, "I saved my great-great-grandpa's life when he fell into the lake."

Ella wrinkled her forehead and countered, "That's not possible! You can do something when you're younger, but not when you're older," she logically reasoned.

"When great-great-grandpa fell off the dock, I saved him," he repeated with unwavering conviction, his pointer finger indicating the spot where the rescue had taken place.

True, I had told him a story. Ford was my maternal grandpa — a farmer, horse lover, school bus driver, and jokester. He didn't have much experience around lakes. In fact, he could not swim, but enjoyed the occasional motor boat ride or sitting with someone holding a fishing pole. On the day I thought for sure he was going to die, I was a youngster sitting on a lawn chair by this very same dock.

Dad, Uncle Merle, and Grandpa were taking the boat out that afternoon. Dad was holding the front end tight to the dock so that Grandpa could get in first. Guess Grandpa missed the lesson on leaning down, holding onto both sides, and distributing his weight. Just as he planted his first foot on the middle seat, a breeze came up, causing the back of the boat to depart from the dock. That jarred Dad's grip loose and the parallel parked boat began to drift away.

Back on shore, we watched, wide-eyed and frozen in place as Grandpa began to do the splits. Remember, this man could not swim and the water at the end of the dock was well over his head. The opportunity to choose between the dock and the boat was quickly passing. Fully clothed and nowhere to go, he lowered his behind toward the water, doing a "reverse" belly flop into the waves with a loud and voluminous splash.

We held our breath behind clenched teeth, watching the spot where he disappeared, down below the lake's surface, just like today's clam. We sat immobile until finally, with a yelp and a gasp, he rose out of the waters, arms flailing, before he got his footing and began wiping the lake from his eyes and nose.

Who was I to question if James had saved his great-great-grandpa "when he was older" as he professed. Do I know what realm we are in before birth? Don't they say that children hold pre-birth knowledge until we socialize them out of it? Studies have been published on kids speaking of things they have no way of knowing, unless...

"James," I began. "I am so glad you didn't let Grandpa Ford drown," I affirmed his claim, hoping he might add more clairvoyant insights from what might be a window into his pre-existence.

He crossed his arms, bobbing his head for emphasis. "When my great-great-grandpa stepped into that boat, it started to float away, he jumped into the lake, and I saved him!"

How could we have known that some entity, a "James-of-the-future," might have boosted non-swimming Ford's head above the water? When Grandpa returned safely into view, were we too relieved to ask him what happened. Instead, we began to laugh, recalling the sight of his splash, forgetting the fear of his fall. Had Grandpa felt a push from "James-of-the-future" that brought his feet to the shallows? The very place where James adamantly points at today insisting:

"I have something to say. It was me. I saved great-great-grandpa."

Merle Iserman gives father-in-law, Ford Wise, a lift

James and the Bungee

*I*f something was amiss, we always wondered if it was James.

When we heard the antique door knob rattling, it was, "James! Stop that! It will break and we won't be able to get out."

When the flashlight was found on the floor surrounded by batteries, it was, "James, come here and put them back inside. We'll need that tonight!"

When Ella and I went to pump water that morning, we saw the bungee cord that holds the pipes together lying on the ground, and we looked for James.

I soon found him and held up the limp cord. He looked at me and back at the dangling bungee and, with the assurance of a seasoned handyman, stated: "You don't need to have it there."

"Well, yes we do," I countered. "It holds the handle in place when we pump water," or so my father had explained to me long ago.

Then, I had a moment of doubt. Was this just another thread of cabin lore that we, unquestionably, followed? Like the warning not to plug in the toaster and coffee pot at the same time or it would blow a fuse. We hadn't blown a fuse in over 25 years, but no one dared test the theory. Could James be right? I looked down at him, ignoring my inner dialogue.

"James, we need the pump to work so that we have water." At least I knew this much to be true.

"You can go and get other water," he assured me.

"If you're thinking of the lake, we don't drink that water, and besides, you're avoiding the bungee situation."

"Can I help you pump water now?" he offered, again side-stepping the issue.

I took the cord in one hand and James by the other and walked back to where Ella was waiting by the pump. I tried multiple times to wind the bungee back into position while the kids stood quietly by until...

"Nana," Ella said excitedly, like she does when she has a bright idea. "Nana, I took a picture of the pump this morning. We could look at it and..."

"Go get it!" I interrupted. "That is brilliant." I was impressed by her eight-year-old technological solution.

With that plan, Ella zoomed the pump picture in close and James guided me until I had the bungee in place. We pumped slowly, as directed by my father's painted instructions on the handle, and the water again flowed into our pail.

As to the cabin lore of the pump needing a bungee – I wonder if James was correct when he told me: "You don't need it!"

Yet, as with so many warnings passed down from my father to me, my grown-up self still doesn't have the nerve to risk taking James', perhaps sage, advice.

Lessons Learned

*F*our extra people visiting added to the total of swimsuits and beach towels that would need room to dry on the short clothesline strung between my metal carport poles. Maybe Grandpa Robert could reinforce the old posts and re-string the plastic cords, resurrecting the former clothes drying area by the garden.

Just as he finished wrapping the cords and tying special Boy Scout knots in place, the swimmers appeared from around the corner, coming up the steps from the lake for lunch. It was then that little James saw his opportunity.

Before Grandpa Robert could yell out, "No, don't!" James burst into a run, took a flying leap, grabbed the line and swung his feet gleefully into the air. This was followed by a resounding "CRACK" as the two vintage posts sagged low, bringing joyous James back to earth with a thud. The delighted look on his face also collapsed. Robert's head shook back and forth, not in disbelief — more like — what next?

I pointed Robert toward the boathouse where the shovels and post-hole digger live. As he turned to go, James brushed himself off and scurried to catch up. "Can I help you, Grandpa Robert?" he pleaded.

Robert shot me a look that clearly translated to, "Could you please find something else for him to do?" I glared back, wide-eyed, jutting my chin toward little James' eager face and sent him a telepathic plea. Here was a four-year-old child, wanting a chance to be with Grandpa and learn how to fix things. Don't blow it!

Robert paused, shrugged his shoulders and called out to James, "Do you think you can carry a shovel?" James took Robert's hand and off they went to the boathouse.

I returned to the cabin kitchen, where I could watch the repair project while I finished making lunch. James was seated by a growing pile of dirt. Sometimes he filled the hole while Grandpa was still digging deeper. Sometimes, he untied the rope that was supposed to be tied. Mostly, he watched each detail, patiently following Grandpa's every move until the project was done.

"Good job, guys!" I shouted out the back door as they returned the tools to the boathouse.

"And, thanks for putting away the tools. Great-great-Grandma Nellie always used to say, 'A place for everything and everything in its place!' Now you'll find them next time you need them." This little piece of family history was aimed at both of them.

James beamed as he proudly dragged the shovel behind him. When Robert passed by, he leaned toward me and whispered, "I could have finished this job in half the time."

My eyes again went wide as I nodded toward James, still savoring their adventure.

"But," Robert quickly interjected, "It was a good learning experience for James."

"Yes," I agreed, adding, "And for somebody else."

The Fort and the Whisk Broom

"*T*hat is my fort," James proclaimed as he headed for the outhouse right before lunch.

The two-holer has a rug, a wall hanging depicting local wildlife, a plaque labeled "Count Your Blessings" that provides a list of good advice while you sit there, a can of Lysol, a yellow waste can complete with a pedal so you can access the lime, a whisk broom, and my dad's sign on the wall behind the two toilet lids reading, "My aim is to keep this bathroom clean. Your aim will help."

Sign inside the outhouse:
"My aim is to keep this bathroom clean. Your aim will help."

The main attraction for James is the string, a multi-choice closure Dad devised by tying loops at different intervals to provide varied light and air options. James, enamored with his fort, often "had to go" so that he could play with the door string.

On this occasion, right before lunch, both James and his sister, Ella, had "to go" at the same time. This should not be a problem with a two-holer, except Ella preferred her privacy. James also had the option of using an appointed "pee-tree" not too far away, but the outhouse was, after all, his fort, and he ran to beat her to its entrance.

However, Ella's scream announced her arrival before he got there, not because she was racing but because, "There's a great, big, black spider in here!"

"Nanaaaaaaa," she wailed. "Come quick!"

"Ella, it's a daddy long-legs, a friendly spider. They don't bite. Most spiders are our friends. See that spider web? It catches the flies that *do* bite us!" I finished, hoping she would see spiders as our allies.

James arrived, breathless, unimpressed with the spider and began to squeeze his way past us into his fort.

They both chose to sit. James seemed to be listening. "I think I'm done," he finally said, "but I didn't hear anything."

"There's no water here," Ella pointed out. "But, it is stinky," she said, grabbing the can of Lysol.

"Just aim it at the seats and not the air," I advised her. "We want to disinfect, not inhale the chemicals!"

With that, James grabbed for the whiskbroom. "I want to clean away this cobweb," he said before I could stop what was about to happen.

He tried to be careful. He really did. He had, with his four-year-old coordination, whisked the spider's web away and was putting the broom back on its ledge. Somehow, it bounced, not once but twice, and hopped right into the open hole vanishing into the darkness below.

Without missing a beat, he said, "I'll go get my flashlight!"

"Eeeuuuu," Ella said, holding her nose.

"Oh, dear," I managed, trying to think fast.

"We'll figure it out after lunch," I began. "Everyone is waiting for us. Grandmère says its disrespectful to the cook to be late."

They raced each other back to the porch, where the family was seated around the table. The screen door barely slapped behind them when the whisk broom adventure spilled out to the assembled in a jumble of interruptions. James then concluded, "Now, we need a flashlight."

To our combined horror, Grandpa Robert responded, "OK. Where is it?"

James ran to get it and Grandpa said he'd be right back.

Not only was it my mother's strict expectation of respect for the cook to be at the table when the food was still hot, but certain topics were not appropriate for mealtime conversation.

"Speaking of the outhouse," she said, trying to steer the topic in another direction. "Who put the stick in the door to help lock it?" expecting to be able to compliment James, for a change.

James was quick to respond. "I didn't do it!" he proclaimed proudly.

"Oh," Grandmère continued. "I thought it was you. You are always figuring things out. I like it."

He put his head down on the table. "Well, this time I didn't do it."

His disappointment was interrupted by Grandpa Robert's triumphant return. "I got it out," he announced to the incredulous diners. "And, it's all cleaned up, good as new!" he looked around the table... for what? Approval?

James looked at Ella. Ella looked at her dad. He looked at his wife. She and I dared not look at Grandmère. I looked back at Robert slowly enunciating my response.

"This cabin is full of re-used, recycled, and re-purposed stuff, but this time, we're in the market for a RE-placement!"

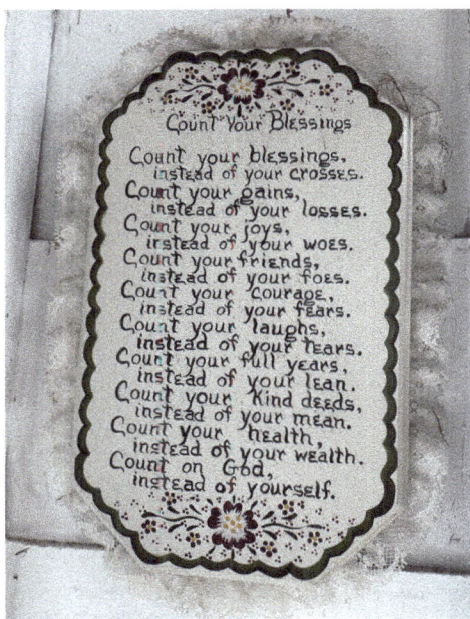

When you sit down in the outhouse, this plaque is on the wall in front of you reminding you to count your blessings.

Ella's privy haiku, 2024

Sprinkle a tinkle
Sit and enjoy the peacefulness
Don't forget the lime

** You add a scoop of lime after using the out house.

Friends

Who's Who in the Guest Book

Guests: Sign here and have an alibi

*O*ne of the first items brought into the new 1957 cabin was the Guest Book. The joke was that by signing your name, date, and comment, you would have an alibi. The real deal was to have a history of guests, their memories, and later, cabin data, such as when the electricity was put in or the green shag rug taken out. Over time, the comments grew longer requiring the addition of Cabin Journa s. These began with phenology, growing to lengthy vignettes.

This expanded to include mini-diaries from the renters, the international guests, and regulars.

Several Guest Books are now filled and stored in the bookcase, ready to reference if we want to verify a date, note climate change, animal and bird sightings, or double-check our commur al memories.

Of the international friends, we have:
1) Rosalia Wong, a Chinese woman we hosted on weekends while a student in Eau Claire. Visited in 1968.
2) Lucia Victoria Sarmiento, from Bogotá, Colombia, an exchange student from Memorial High School. Visited in 1969.
3) Clive, Rita, Jason, and Kylie from Switzerland — met Clive and Rita in Morocco, 1976. Visited in 1990.

4) Carlos Corona, Culiacan, Mexico, son of Polo and Teresita, whose older sons, Polin and Fife, had been exchange students in Brainerd. Visited in 1998.

5) Maribel Adame, my forever amiga from Spain, visited after a 40-year wait! Visited in 2017.

6) Fabienne Garnier, France, one time Amity Aide in Brainerd. We also visited her in France. Visited in 2018.

The regular registered guests included my father's hunting friends, rental families from college days, and outdoorsmen. My mom invited couples for weekends, forays of hiking for the women and fishing for the men. Her favorite entertainment became the Northernaire's Showboat "Off the Las Vegas beat" act – Skip Wagner – known for his off-color jokes and playing two trumpets simultaneously. At this writing, he is alive and his statue can be found in downtown Three Lakes. Sadly, the Oneida Village, where the statue resided, burned down a few years ago.

Then, there is Lois. Lovely, amazing, funny, Mistress of game playing, friend since Hamline days and our studies in Seville, Spain, Lois. That Lois. She recites poetry from Ogden Nash to Mary Oliver. Her journal comments remind us of the importance of commas and her long, winding jokes have punchlines like: Yeast is yeast and Vest is Vest and ne'er the Mane shall Tweet.

Guest Books and Journals record life lessons, births and deaths, noted by the appearance and disappearance of their signatures, leaving a trace of their thoughts and character on the pages.

Ironically, Jim Doth penned: "Live and Learn, Die and Forget it all. Aspire to inspire before you expire."

Little Life Lessons

"What gets your attention gets you."

"You are what you eat, and so it is with your mind. Garbage in, garbage out."

"Prior proper planning prevents piss poor performance."

- Donald Kurtz

"... an abundance of caution." - Phyllis Kurtz

"Did you ever think that the whole purpose of your life might be to serve as a warning to others?" - Lois Hollingsworth

Janet, Lois, Avery, and Ella at Girls' Camp
Current and future wild women of the woods

The Clive and Rita Payne family from Switzerland, 1990

Clive with his first real life car hop, 1990

Phyllis, Maribel (from Spain), and Lois, 2017

Phyllis with "Dusty" Dan and
Judy Davis, 2019

Memories

Fabienne from France, 2018

Charlie and Kay (Iserman) Geguzis, 2023

Lois in her Seuss-tastic t-shirt, 2019

Dave and Val Goeke family, 2022

Wise Cracks and Wisdom

*R*on and Reg Goeke were also from the WISE side of the family. After filling me in on the fate of recent Illinois governors spending time "making license plates" after bouts of corruption, Ron paused and pointed out, "Some people just make a poor choice of ancestors."

Grandpa Ford Wise used to eat a cookie with milk after breakfast. Sometimes, he'd eat an extra cookie. Then, he would have to put a little more milk in his glass. "I have to make these things come out even!" he would say, as he continued to take another helping. When finally finished, he'd push his chair away from the table, declaring, "Plenty, plenty, plenty," before announcing, "I'm headed off to amputate a whisker."

"Horrors!" Phyllis Kurtz's favorite exclamation, implemented after startling or bad news.

"Lips that touch wine will never touch mine." Grandma Edith
(Yet Grandpa always added Rum to the eggnog at Christmas.)

"Your Body is Your Temple," is my preferred mantra, especially repeated to Greg during his teenage years.

"Have another brownie," Grandma Edith invited, coming around with the platter yet again. Edith had diabetes, but loved to bake. During visits, she offered my brother and me an array of sweets, despite warnings not to eat too much sugar. Watching her stick a needle of insulin in her thigh every morning was a more vivid warning. On the other side of the family, Floyd Kurtz had the occasional diabetic episode, requiring Nellie to grab a Hershey bar from the stash, used in case of this emergency. The specter of diabetic genetics hovered over every meal. Health is the foundation for everything.

"Cleanliness is close to godliness," lives in my head. I found that works much better if you live alone.

Sayings go inter-generational — if shared. They are golden nuggets of personal character or cultural wealth. Handing them down is a treasure. Adding new ones is a treat. Pay attention and pick up some new gems and pass them on. This is my most recent. I plan to incorporate it soon!

A new one for the future from Rebecca Timmons, taken from an AAUW meeting discussing a fundraiser:

"The juice isn't worth the squeeze."

And most recently, from 2024, shared with us by Lois and her German friend when the easement papers were finally signed, when we added:

"Lid shut, monkey dead."

Eastern Philosophy

Lao Tzu wisdom recorded in one of THE CABIN JOURNALS

"Watch your thoughts;
they become your words.
Watch your words;
they become your actions.
Watch your actions;
they become your habits.
Watch your habits;
they become your character.
Watch your character;
it becomes your destiny."

James had a thought... and it became his character.

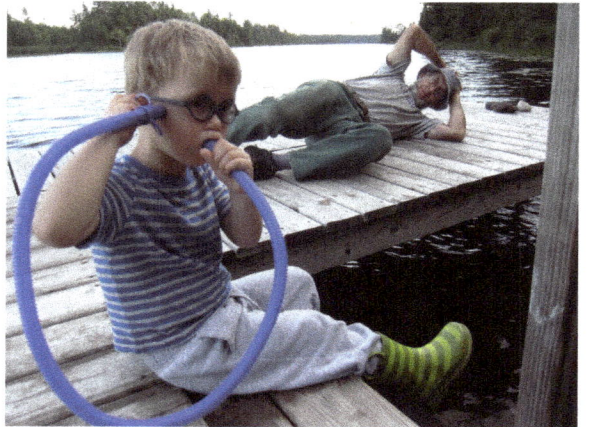

James talking to himself as Grandpa Robert looks on.
You don't have to buy expensive toys to entertain a kid.

I end with my dad's Protestant Rosary. Donald was known for his "prayer without ceasing" in his later years. As a one-time pastor, he had his favorites. He began to refer to his "Protestant Rosary" which combined the Beatitudes (Matthew 5: 1-12) plus the Lord's Prayer (Matthew 6: 9-13).

3   Blessed are the poor in spirit,
     for theirs is the Kingdom of Heaven.
4   Blessed are those who mourn,
     for they will be comforted.
5   Blessed are the meek,
     for they will inherit the Earth.
6   Blessed are those who hunger and thirst for righteousness,
     for they will be satisfied.
7   Blessed are the merciful,
     for they will be shown mercy.
8   Blessed are the pure in heart,
     for they will see God.
9   Blessed are the peacemakers,
     for they will be called the Sons of God.
10   Blessed are those who are persecuted because of
     righteousness, for theirs is the Kingdom of Heaven.
11   Blessed are you when people insult you, persecute you and
     falsely say all kinds of evil against you because of Me.
12   Rejoice and be glad, because great is your reward in heaven,
     for in the same way they persecuted the prophets who were
     before you...

AMEN

You Can Never Have Too Many Chairs

"You can never have too many chairs," is what Lois said as we perused the annual Fleazaar at Mercer, Wisconsin, in the furniture building.

We discovered Fleazaar through my dear relative, Charles Laible. He was supposed to be our neighbor at Lake Julia, but fate wasn't having it. I'll call him up and get the exact notes, but the gist is that he and his wife, Carol, were going to buy the Point property. Charles and Carol often visited my parents and loved our cabin, so much so that, when Ed put his place up for sale, they made an offer. This is when it gets fuzzy. They were on their way north with a down payment when Ed Zager (or his realtor) raised the price, not once, but twice. The second time it put the property out of their range, ending them in Mercer at another cabin. This is where we caught up with Charles at his church's Fleazaar, quite the event in the woods each third Wednesday of July.

Lois was already an aficionada of thrifting, so it took no persuasion to get her interested. A field behind the local airport takes most of the parking away from the highway. The church and outbuildings are organized by topic; water crafts are lined up outside — pontoons, canoes, kayaks, and all the gear are there. Sheds protect bedding, games, toys, tackle, and tools from sun or rain. The antiques are displayed with the handicrafts, you get the idea. It is a Thrifter heaven.

Charles is the bike-seller, has been for some 25-years. He sells dozens — all sizes, colors, and reasonably priced. He sits alongside the fleet leaned up by the church and waits for offers. While he waits, it gives us time to visit. You see, he lives in Illinois and this twist of fate brought him, his family, and now many members of the Dakota Presbyterian church to this neck of the woods each summer. So, it worked out well for the Laibles, the Goekes, and other distant relatives. But, my mom never totally forgave Ed for his treason, depriving us from having family on the lake. More than once, I heard her sigh, "If Charles was at that cabin, you would have a whole generation of your peers to help you and be your family."

Perhaps the universe has a sense of humor, or at least a sense of irony. While standing in the cemetery outside of Dakota, where we had just interred my mother that summer of 2021, some of us walked to the edge of the field where the "Goeke" cows were coming to the fence to check out the activities. The topic turned to the cabins at Julia and Mercer. Without much hesitation, Dave Goeke asked about visiting at Julia with some of his family.

All the sorrow of being a recent and aging orphan, lifted. I wasn't alone. I had family in Illinois, even though they weren't at the end of my lane. Turns out I have Dave, Val, and their grandkids. I have Andy and maybe soon, Jim. It turns out that folks don't love my outhouse, but will come anyway. They want to kayak, fish, and swim to grass island and float in the big tubes!

Guess it's time to get some more chairs.

You know, "You can never have too many chairs!"

Jan's Fleazaar find, 2022

Lois talked me into buying this chair at Fleazaar, 2022

A thank you gift from Chip Borkenhagen for editing Jan's first book. This is a warning for fishermen in Lake Julia.

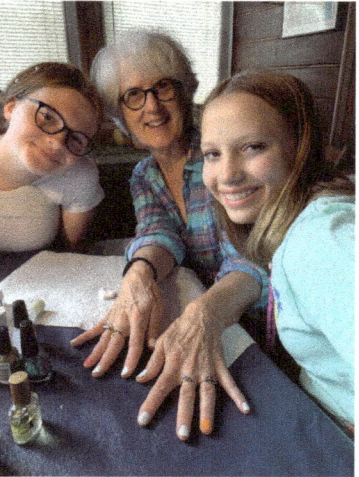

A girlie-girl moment at Girls' Camp

The pool table legacy...

Ed Zager, age 50, and Greg Doth, age 2, in the 1970s, try their luck at pool. The pool table has been inherited from one generation to the next. Unfortunate y, James has allergies and Jan has to vacuum it before use.

The Other Cabin
(On the Point)

There was another cabin in the Kurtz history – the palisade cabin on the Point. The story is recorded in Donald Kurtz's letters describing how his North Central professor, Dr. Harr, and wife, Juanita, owned the peninsula. A wind storm provoked their need for clean-up help and the invite to some students to "go north" and join their cleaning team. Ed Zager and my dad, Donald, answered the call.

The upshot was a partnership, buying approximately 52 acres and the vintage cabin, with its great room, furnished with a long table, some chairs, a trundle bed for kiddos and a few sectioned off rooms for private sleeping and storage. This was shared by Ed, his wife, Ginny, their two daughters, Peggy and Judy, and the four of us. Occasionally, the parents of both Ed (Alma and Herb) and Donald (Nellie and Floyd) were added. In 1957, the overflow moved my father to pursue a partnership/land split resulting in two properties going into the present.

As a child, I only have images left by black and white photos of the time. My brother and I were bathed in a large dish pan. I am a toddler being held by my mother in a fishing boat. My father holds my hand as I learn to walk in the shallows of the lake. My grandpa Kurtz holds a stringer of fish as he poses in front of his, likely 1940s, car. Grandma Nellie holds baby Stevie on her ample lap as she relaxes in a rocker. These were taken before the 1957 move.

The next set of photos show horses at work with Dad and his building crew, pulling logs. The original two-handed saws are on display in the current porch. A bulldozer made the cut into the esker's hillside. Blocks are set for the raising of the new cabin. By 1957, there are family photos of Keith Wise, his wife Rachel, and my cousins, Linda, Kathy, and Kim, standing in front of a cabin shell receiving its first guests, yet far from being finished.

From those days until Ed sold his place in 1993, each summer was filled with memories carried into the present – by me, by Judy and Peggy, by the Wes Norton family, friends of both families who rented, and the kids from South Milwaukee who came "up" for Ed's canoe camps. Enter Richard Urban, the only man to spend an entire winter at the Kurtz cabin.

Yes, the canoe camps. My next story tells of the summer my parents allowed me to spend two weeks at the Point Cabin during Ed's infamous "Canoe Camps" – one week each with a weekend in between – a weekend where Judy and I were allowed to stay alone at the Point Cabin while he switched out campers. A weekend when Nortons, with their teenaged children, were renting.

A weekend when the bears were in the woods. Judy and I were 14.

Canoe Camp
Brought to you by Rev. Edward Zager

*B*arely a teenager, I wasn't tuned into the back story of Ed's Canoe camp offerings. I do remember being shipped to South Milwaukee where I was then turned around to go north with Ed, likely in his turquoise IH (International Harvester) truck, a predecessor to the present day SUV. I was stuffed in the back with his daughter Judy and a batch of city kids. Let the games begin!

The National Forest Service road, the two precarious hills leading to the cabins' lanes, the towering pine, and finally the sparkling lake were home to us, but not so to Ed's teen city campers. We literally bounced and tumbled as Ed took the long hill, careened into the hairpin turn at the top, slamming us into each other as his belly laugh filled the car. The aged Palisade cabin came into sight, just before the peninsula, called The Point, reached into the lake.

Once parked, the backpacks, supplies, and achy bodies were carted inside. The floorplan was a basic long room with kitchen at one end and a variety of chairs at the big window on the other end facing lakeside. There was a basement below with extra beds and a walk out exit to The Point. Ed quickly directed girls below and announced that the boys would be camping on the island, just a few minutes row over the lily pads.

Chores were divided without thought to gender. Everyone had KP (kitchen patrol) including pumping our water, setting tables, cooking, and clean-up. The loose schedule included work times – stacking firewood, cleaning the beach area, sweeping the cabin floor; lake time for swimming and canoes; outdoor games such as Capture the Flag and Kick the Can; and evening vespers around the camp fire. Judy and I were in our realm, excelling with canoes and tramping through the woods – our childhood backyard.

Capture the Flag gave us a chance to shine in our knowledge of the terrain. The cabin lane ran the backbone of the esker ridge becoming the "No Man's Land" – the communal safe area for each team. One side of the esker dipped into a swampy bog and the other down to the lake, forming distinct team areas to be protected. Oh, the joy of running the length of the lane, exit through the forest to the bottom of the hill, grab the flag, and know a secret way back up and over to one's own turf – thus winning again! Judy and I were already entering the age of feminism, experiencing special glee when outrunning and outwitting the boys.

Besides outdoor running games, Ed provided a canoe trip to the next lake in the chain, Virgin, thus giving these forays into his woods the name: Canoe Camp. Before taking the campers on the two-hour creek trek, all participants had to pass the canoe test. Not everyone was a good swimmer, but the real test was to flip the canoe, get it back upright and crawl back in. The 16 to 18-foot Grumman canoes were aluminum, but heavy. Even Judy and I were challenged by this rite of passage, despite having taken the trip numerous times.

The canoe trips always involved a number of races, water fights, and other shows of competition between guys and girls. It was a sign of weakness if a girl would scream when a spider got knocked off an overhanging branch into the canoe. It was a sign of strength to douse the passing canoe with paddles full of spray. The end game was to be the first to reach the island across the lake at Virgin and set up the picnic. (Yes — a Virgin Island.) The pines rose high even then, occasionally hosting an eagle's nest. There was a sand beach on one end and "iceberg" boulders on the other, their tops rising just above the water with wide slimy sides reaching down to the bottom. We weren't the first, nor the last, to picnic here as the sun filtered through the branches to the pine needle floor. This canoe trip was the highlight, but not the only excursion.

There was also the hike to the fire tower, now long since dismantled. Ed, forever the woodsman guide, organized our group of hikers and headed down the lane. After passing the Kurtz cabin, the road returned to the creek via the two "monster" hills and back into Nicolet National Forest land. Before reaching the public road, we veered off to explore the remains of Sheltered Valley Ski area, a place of some fame in the 50s. A man named Carl Marty brought his dream of the Northernaire and the Sheltered Valley Ski area to folks in Chicago and made quite a living.

This trail was previously the access for the workers going to the top of the ski lifts on a half dozen hills ranging from beginner to what was, for the area — the high hill, not to be compared with the Rockies! Its popularity required a major upgrade of the once rutted logging road to allow passage of buses carrying in the skiers who stayed at the Northernaire. Taking this access lane leads hikers along the top of all the ski runs with a view of the Chalet across the valley. Cy Williams, a ball player of national fame turned architect/builder, designed the lodge, complete with dining area and large windows for viewing all downhill activity. The park in Three Lakes is named after him.

Our trail hike led us side-stepping down the steeper hill, across the opening, and up to the ledge, where the abandoned chalet stood until the Forest Service dismantled it due to vandalism. Ed gathered us there before announcing that we would leave the paths and continue through the forest to the fire tower beyond. We were to follow him in single file and not dally. I marveled at how he picked his way through the underbrush, over downed logs, noted that the north side of trees had the moss – a clue for hikers without compasses, and led us into the opening where the tower rose vicariously into the sky. How did he do it? Not get lost? Years later he pointed out the electrical lines that hid in the trees, a perfect clue leading him directly to the tower.

The metal structure had stairs surrounded by a protective circle of steel that, if an adult, one could lean back on for rest or protection when climbing. The small office-like edifice at the top was locked, only for use by a bonafide ranger with binoculars. One by one, we were given the chance to ascend as far up as we felt able, each step taking us to and then above the treetops. The stair steps were narrow and spaced a tad far apart for my comfort. The wind blew through the open tube. Judy and I were bound to get to the top. It was, literally, breathtaking!

I don't remember how many of us were in this first week of camp. I only remember two by name, Richard and his cousin, Jan. Richard was a quiet, already tall, lanky teenager and his cousin, somewhat the opposite. She was older, chatty, shorter, and slightly rounded. I suppose, due to his size, he was expected to do more physical labor. I suppose, due to his gender, he

was expected to be stoic and strong. I was unaware that his father had died earlier and that Ed had often been there for his family. Ed was now shepherding the two north, for a change. Canoe camp living was, in fact, a life-changer.

In 2002 canoe camp buddies, Richard, Jan, and Judy (Ed's daughter), were reunited to celebrate the life of Ed at the Carol and Harold Zager property at the upper end of Lake Julia.

"A time to weep, a time to dance, a time for every season under heaven."

The Weekend
Judy and Jan - Alone in the Woods?

The week ended, but my friendships with Richard and Jan continued. That is another story. For this moment, Judy and I were given the unexpected gift of freedom. We were only 14 when we watched the South Milwaukee kids pack back into the IH and bump down the lane. We were on our own... but not exactly alone.

The Norton family was renting the Kurtz cabin, so there was no cause for concern or parental neglect. Wes and Dottie had some kids, two of whom were about our age. Dave and, yes, another Judy, were seasoned Lake Julia kids, as their parents were regulars at my family's place.

We were also signed up to spend an afternoon with the Yenerichs and Busaccas at Deer Lake. The adventures were on. First, because a bear was sighted during this time period and second, there were boys involved.

My father, Donald, Judy's father, Ed, and aforementioned George Yenerich and Whitey Busacca, were all classmates at the Evangelical Theological Seminary in Naperville, Illinois. Judy and I were picked up to spend the afternoon with their families, likely a good way to keep us safe. Well, nobody had mentioned these families both had boys... our age. Enter Alan and Paul.

Yes, there were other kids, but it was years later before I was reunited with Ann and got the backstories filled in. That afternoon, the focus was on a marvelous rope swing, hanging from a tall tree and stretching out over the lake. It required climbing a ladder, grabbing a rope with a small wooden plank seat, jumping into the air, and landing with one leg on either side of the rope. Depending on the exertion, one might fly out over the water more than once before letting go the rope, splashing down with a scream.

After mastering that, we entered the second phase of rope swinging — involving two people! On the return swing, person #2 would grab the rope and land in your lap for the second trip out over the lake. This was both terrorizing and exhilarating! Oh my, the yellling, the splash, the attempt not to land on each other. Oh, the fun. When Judy and I left that day, she couldn't stop talking about Alan and I couldn't quit thinking about Paul.

But, what of Dave, back at the cabin. He and his sister spent some time with us, including telling bear stories. We had been back and forth down the lane and glad for that friendship. Being on our own was fine, but having the Nortons close by was comforting. And now we were faced with our first night alone in the cabin. Or, not.

Judy and I doubted that our request would be granted, but we wanted Dave to stay overnight. We were aware this might sound strange, if not brash. Plus, it required the agreement of parents and his willingness to be our knight in shining armor. We really didn't want to be considered whimpy, yet it would be reassuring if he came over, moved the bed in front of the door, and slept there. To our surprise and relief, the request was granted. Dave showed up after supper. He helped us move the bed in position — sideways, across the door, thus giving the most coverage. To my recall, Judy and I slept soundly. I don't recall if Dave was so fortunate.

Addendum:

Since my Camp Fire Girls counselor set us up with pen pals for 25¢ an address, I've been an enthusiastic letter-writer. During this particular summer, I became "pen pals" with Richard, Jan, Dave, and Alan.

A few years later, I was invited to South Milwaukee to be a bridesmaid in Jan's wedding with Richard as my accompanying groomsman. I met the whole family. The Norton family continued to rent until the parents passed. Later, on occasion, the "kids" rented, bringing their next generation to the Kurtz cabin.

Judy Zager ceased cabin visits when her dad sold the place in 1993.

Richard holds the honor of being the only human to spend a full winter at the Kurtz cabin — logging out the spruce-budworm. Richard and I continue to be "life-long" friends. He loves the place, almost as much as I do.

Richard joins Don and Jan for his annual visit

Ann (Yenerich) Essig (Alan's sister) reunited with Jan in 2021

Changes

When the Cabin is Mine

First published in *Her Voice*, Fall 2010

F inally! Finally, I am swaying lazily back and forth in the canopied swing on the shores of Lake Julia, where green grasses and orange hawkweed bow their heads slightly in the lake scented breeze.

This is my second week here as the 'new owner' of my parent's cabin; a cabin originally laid out with tape measure and string in an Illinois cornfield over 50 years ago. A cabin brought to life by my father, his father, an uncle, and a cadre of friends in the once wilds of northern Wisconsin. A cabin cobbled together over time between whims and good deals.

Dad liked to point to the boat house and remind us, "This used to be our garage on Rudolph Road..." Or, as we grab the porch railing, "That came from the old rental property." Neat stacks of cannibalized boards await their future possibilities outside the boathouse, while inside straightened nails are organized in plastic bins of appropriate sizes. The cabin is a culmination of hammering, mowing, tree removal, scraping, shellacking, lane upkeep, interspersed with some fishing and hunting.

Until this year, my cabin experience reflected forests full of deer trails, hours of floating over lily pads in my inner-tube, kayaking to the next lake, blueberry pancakes, and late night Scrabble. When dad turned 80, he began to take me on the journey of timber management, taxes, signing checks, and meeting local handymen, for yet unknown, maintenance needs.

In April, the paperwork made the cabin officially 'mine.' A mere week later, the phone rang as I entered the house, exhausted after a particularly long work week. "The lane flooded," Russ, the lakes' handyman reported. "The beaver dammed the culvert. The upper lane washed out. I pulled out the sticks. What do you want me to do with the road?" Ay! Baptism by beavers!

Two months later, I sit here, watching the fluffy white clouds appear from behind the esker ridge as they parade themselves out over the lake where Mom and I call out their shapes. Not so on the day I arrived.

It was pouring. My plan to mow and open the cabin before the arrival of my parents washed away in a hypothermic deluge. Thanks to my dad's closing-up procedures, there was dry firewood inside. I lit the fire, opened the rooms for heating and headed out to pump water. It was there I noticed a large red, dead spruce leaning precariously over the bank toward the lake. The voice in my head, clearly my father's, started a 'to do' list. Duly noted, I finished filling the stove containers and kitchen pails and returned them to the cabin. That completed, I changed into dry bedclothes, slipped between the army blankets, and called it a day.

Morning came in cold and gray. Good day to start up the mower and weed whip. Or could I? Following dad's teachings, I checked the gas, the oil, the spark plugs, but the yanking of the cord to right field only resulted in a very sore arm. The next logical move: sit down in the grass and cry! Which, I wouldn't have done, had I not also noticed the flat tire on the trailer. Enough! I returned to the cabin kitchen, took out the yellow legal pad and started: 'The List.'

Let's see. Dad wanted the kitchen floor jacked up and leveled from the crawl space. The tarped car port needed to be dismantled and replaced. Any dead spruce should be cut before the budworm spread. Add to that a mower and weed whip that wouldn't work, plus that flat tire and, oh yes, the small dock is smashed to bits. Probably by ice!

Dad, who had just had a pacemaker put in a fortnight before, arrived that afternoon. We walked the grounds together. He talked me through removal and cleaning of spark plugs, indicated the line of labeled red gas cans (motor boat, weed whip, chainsaw), and took out the jack and boards before we headed up the steep hill to the flat trailer tire. I looked at him, restricted by the doctor (no heavy work or lifting) and by the passing of years (memory, strength, endurance). I looked at myself, not a person constructed for reaching high places, nor toting large loads! By the end of day one, I was aware of much more that I could NOT do than that which I could... But hey... I could... Call Russ!

In one morning, the floor was level, the tree was down, the kayak dock straightened, the tire changed. (My jack had broken! Such was my strength!) Sauntering toward me, wiping his hands on his jeans, he asked dryly, "So, what else is on The List?"

"Well," I responded, "Dad would like the canoe moved to the lakeside of the boat house and wants you to look at some stumps."

As Russ and I each took an end of the weighty 1968, 18-foot Grumman, he interjected, "What about the carport? Have you decided?"

I glanced over at Dad for direction. "It is your place," he said for the third time that morning.

Dad had single-handedly assembled this 'good deal' years ago. Now, the bent, rusty poles were loosely covered by ratty tarps! He had supervised Mom and I, as we crazy-quilted together various sized canvases with an even greater array of bungee cords. I was elected to teeter on a decaying step ladder, which Mom held to steady on the slant, while I attempted to hook cords to just out-of-range posts. The bungees and my patience nearly snapped. There was no point in asking why he didn't just have one big tarp. After all, this would do perfectly well!

But, and I quote, "It is my place now." Within five minutes, I had ordered the goods and Russ left for his front-end loader to even out the platform. By the end of the second day, he had graded the washed out road, picked up the carport materials, and completed its construction! After laying the last stone on the base, he again approached me, "What else is on The List?"

"Well, there is the replacement of the broken gate," I ventured. A tree had smashed the old one beyond repair. I could see Dad leaving the dock and heading up the path. I nudged Russ toward his truck hoping he'd get going before Dad would reach us with something new for The List.

Behind me, the kayak gently rocked on the waves. My writing lay dormant in my backpack. The resident phoebe was busily constructing a nest on my bedroom window ledge, dripping moss and mud down the cabin siding. As Russ's truck disappeared over the hilltop, I saw my dad stooping to lift a log that he shouldn't! Inside the kitchen, the sound of the water dipper clanked on its bucket. Mom was making lunch.

That afternoon, Russ' daughter joined him as a go-fer. On a momentary break, she rushed to the dock with her minnow net, dipping it into the sun sparkled waves. I put down my shovel and joined her. We lay on our bellies, counting the pan fish under the dock as we wadded up tiny bread balls to drop in front of their noses. The sun warmed our backs. Then, her father called. I watched her run to him, my breath taken by a pang of *déjà vu*.

I looked over at my father, shoulders hunched, as he shuffled along the pine needle path, propped up by his rake, eyes sweeping the ground. His tan workpants (over 30 years old, he'll proudly tell you), are rolled and cuffed above the ankle. They sport a lighter colored tan patch pocket and black yarn seams mended around the belt. He leans on the rake as he squats to move a rock to the ledge wall. When he straightens up, I have arrived at his side with a sketch of the gate I designed for the lane. I present it to him, with a deep-seated daughterly desire for encouragement.

With tired eyes and perhaps, a sad smile, he nods approvingly, then motions to the round metal table by the woodpile, whose paint is cracking off in large, crispy yellow chips. He clears his throat, pauses, then looks back at me inquiring,

"So, what do you think you'll do with that table?"

Meet Russ
A Man of Few Words and Many Talents

*R*uss stands next to his truck, muscular tattooed arms folded across his broad chest, lips pursed as he scans my premises each year at cabin opening. He is there to put in the dock, clean the gutters, and see if I've concocted any construction projects. After a handshake, he grunts, "Where's the list?" – our inside joke.

Russ is an artist. He painted our cabin sign, paints old saws, and painted the cabin – twice. He also does chainsaw statues. He has a chainsaw carved bear by the turnaround at his place.

Russ usually uses his chainsaw to get me into my cabin driveway. Each season, he enters first, cutting fallen trees, throwing downed limbs back into the woods and later returns with a pole saw for our annual walk about. I point and he trims the dipping pine branches to above head level for when he rides his mower along the east and west walking paths.

Russ is a top tier mechanic. His garage is a shop where vintage cars come back to life. Their internal organs and outside bodywork

are feats of re-incarnation. I'm afraid to breathe around their shiny exteriors and would not think of sitting in one.

Russ builds houses. His own and his neighbor's. He does tiles, roofs, siding, painting entire buildings (along with his art), puts in railings, digs post holes, reupholsters dining room chairs (with the vintage loon curtains in my case), and configures wooden steps to the beach.

Russ is an inventor. He puts grates in entryways so that the dirt gets brushed off shoes before getting into the house. He has a mouse trap that, in his words, will max out at 50 mice. He brought by a five-gallon bucket with an aluminum can poked through with a small metal rod running between the sides. He puts some water in the bottom, peanut butter on the pop can, and sets it on the porch for when I am gone. In the winter, just add antifreeze.

Russ, I reiterate, is a man of few words. After we've checked the items off my list, we go inside for rhubarb cake and milk. I let him cut his piece and put out a gallon of milk with a tall glass.

Russ, it turns out, is a matchmaker. During one of our Rhubarb reunions, my friend, Lois, was along. In between bites, he looked at her and said, "Are you married?" Her blatant response, "No, my husband is dead." Without blinking, he continued, "I have a neighbor you should meet." And, as they say, "The rest is history."

Now for an extraordinary spurt of verbiage, a text message from Russ, who seems to have a good command of adjective, when so moved. When describing a request to take out a nearby pier, he texted: "I would rather have to tunnel out of prison than wrestle with that heavy iron contraption he calls a pier. The lead egghead at a pier design company must have come up with that nightmare. Who else would think that a pier should weigh more than a jumbo jet airplane."

Russ enhanced the family sign with his painting

Menards Carport 1999 upgraded by Russ in 2009

Russ used the vintage curtains to reupholster the entire set of six chairs with the Duncan Phife dining room set

Cindy Joins the Family Litany

*T*he photo shows my grandmother Nellie standing over the cabin kitchen stove, wooden spoon stirring in the soup pot. Her adult daughter, Wilma, helps make breakfast on the newly acquired gas stove. Soon. her husband, Floyd, will pass by with a wash basin and towel, being caught for all time. It is 1957.

The companion photo shows my mother, standing by the table where my brother, Steven, eats. The loft is not yet built. A gas refrigerator replaced the ice box from the old Point cabin. Ice chunks once were cut from the ake and put in the ice house with sawdust and chipped off as needed. When opening the cabin, my father used to scare the bejeebers out of us when preparing to light the gas stove and refridgerator!

Dad would rally us outside and take us midway up the hill, then return to the gas canister outside the kitchen window. With a few turns and twists, a hiss announced the release of the gas into the small piping. Timing was everything. He'd rush back inside, grab the box of matches, hunch down in front of the stove, and then the refrigerator. He had a length of metal with a clip on the end, where the match snapped into place. Once lit, he crouched down low and eased the match into the back of the broiler and waited. If placed correctly, a pop and a whish indicated the stove had been lit. Then, over to the refrigerator. Once completed, he'd return to the hill and announce that it was, again, safe to enter the cabin. At least ice houses never exploded!

Over time, the appliances and the people in the kitchen changed out. Grandma Nellie and Grandma Edith made way for my mother, Phyllis. Phyllis was meticulous in her meal planning, plotting out her menus and making lists of ingredients, packing boxes from home, and leaving the fresh produce for the local grocery store.

The first was Eaglesham's Trading Post by Virgin Lake. Then there was a Bell's grocery near town, which was later sold to Al Yenerich, a family friend. He called it "Al's" after... himself. Several others also tried their hand and gave the grocery store their names. However, it is now called The Town Market, doing its best to provide staples and keep people from driving to Trig's in Eagle River. We always preferred to support the locals and the guy who brought in sweet corn, tomatoes, and fresh fruits in season. He sold his produce out of his truck on the corner of the Winery parking lot, the main intersection in town.

My mom supplemented her breakfasts with the raspberries and blackberries we picked along the lane. If we found enough, she made pies. She set a full table for lunches and suppers, often putting the entrée on a platter to be served family style. The peas, carrots, salads, and bread all had their individual bowls, often dating to her mother's table, once used in Illinois. Mom wore an apron, as did the generation before her — full body, with pockets used to stuff her Kleenex.

The family cuisine and fancy supper dishes fell out of practice when I arrived in the kitchen. I did not make menus but randomly purchased ingredients, often of tomato origin. Chili, spaghetti, Spanish

Rice, lasagna (frozen), taco salads. I was not interested in spending time in a kitchen on a perfectly good day. Calculating the time to meal plan, shop, wash and chop veggies, cook, set table, eat, pump water for doing dishes, put everything away was, in my opinion, better spent floating in a kayak.

To my great fortune, Cindy came into my life. My son brought many friends to the cabin during his youth. There was little Sammy, who talked and walked in his sleep, requiring he bunk downstairs, not in the loft. There was Eddie, invited mostly to play Dungeons and Dragons (D&D), Greg's grand plan but irritating to his grandparents. There was his cousin, Jake, later to grow up and be a guide in Alaska. Once out of high school, Greg invited college friends, and girls entered the picture. That worked pretty well except once, when I arrived to find the remains of a charred pizza in the oven. The clean-up was lovingly done by his grandma, Phyllis.

My father, Don, made a list of cabin clean-up pinned to the wall for check-off. Mostly it directed visitors on how to make a fire (complete with drawn instructions), how to gently use the pump (there was a sign on the fridge about "Jerks" jerking the pump handle), reminders to turn down the draft on the wood stove, and turn off the electricity when shutting down the cabin. It was risky, but they allowed their grandson leeway as part of his growing up experience.

That brings us back to Cindy. When Greg invited Cindy to come "up" to the cabin, it was different. Cindy came from a camping family. Her whole family had worked at Yellowstone one summer. Or, was it two? Cindy didn't whine about mosquitoes — she sprayed. Cindy knew about camp cooking from tacos in a bag to grilling. Cindy planned her menus, packed and labeled her bins, and kept the fish worms separate.

Inviting someone to the cabin was a natural sorting out process. Rites of passage included putting worms on a hook, swimming in a lake with weeds, building campfires, hiking through biting insects, and playing the Simpson's Game of Life, for starters. Cindy did not have to pretend, as she morphed into the next member of our family. She had it covered! She came with her fishing rod, tackle box, ingredients for S'mores, and sat with Greg at the card table at lake's edge to play D&D, something I never got my head around. She would give things

a chance, but not succumb to doing something, just because Greg liked it, a foible of my dating days. I need not have worried. Cindy was her own woman and Greg was beyond lucky.

Greg not only invited her to the cabin, but to join the two of us on our trip to Italy. I had imagined a mother/son bonding moment, but he was serious. Arrangements were made and, on the Isle of Capri, he came off the balcony one morning and introduced Cindy as the future Mrs. Doth. He was beaming and I was released from my promise not to say anything. I was delighted and relieved.

I was deeply touched when Greg announced he'd like to have the wedding at the cabin. It was a testament to his love for this place, the "heart of my soul" and the family treasure. As wonderful as his

wanting to be married in this sacred place of family gathering, I found myself talking him out of it – not that Cindy wouldn't have pointed out the logistics and her own wishes. Later, destination weddings to

Cancun and far-flung islands would become popular, but our vintage cabin didn't have parking, pre-paid all-inclusive packages, nor indoor plumbing. Note that Cindy found a lovely venue closer to home, hired a wedding planner, and, at rehearsal, directed us all when the planner was a no-show. Dad, who was already concerned about his memory, nervously agreed to be one of two pastors, blessing them both with the deepest of grandfatherly love.

Fast forward. Cindy orchestrated a move, which involved driving the moving van from St. Louis Park to Otsego, about 30 miles north. She wisely bought a camper to "get her husband off of the ground" and "out of his recurring nightmare" of camping at Cloud Peak — think tiny tent clinging to the side of the mountain during an all day sleet storm, backpacking out to save our lives. Cindy sewed the cabin's new curtains out of scraps found in the dressers. Cindy is the mother of Ella and James,  a baby that came into the world with Pierre Robins, his jaw needing immediate surgery so that he could breathe and eat. For six weeks, he could not go home. She held him, got the special bottle, stayed through surgeries, holding hands with my son and their daughter, sending them back home while she stayed with James. Kudos to Greg as he kept the proverbial home fires burning.

Today, summer is still a few months off. Cindy texted about cabin dates. She has to reserve vacation time at the office. They are booking weekends of camping in State Parks. There will be a concert in Milwaukee, maybe a chance to swing by northern Illinois to touch base with our relatives. And, maybe late July or early August they could swing by the cabin.

She will make her menus. We will split the grocery-shopping. I will have fresh foods in the fridge and fresh sheets on the beds. She will pack the car and I will mow the lawn. She will drive while Greg navigates and hands snacks to the kids in the backseat. This year, Ella will be 15 in April and James 11 in June.

I used to wait for their arrival with my mom and dad. Then, just with my mom — oh how we would scurry around to make everything perfect. Oh, how we'd pray for good weather and no bugs. Now, I wait alone. I put out a disclaimer on the weather: I am not responsible. I've vacuumed off the kid pool table so James' allergies won't be so bad. I set up the loft for Ella, now considered her room. I'll let Greg have the window seat for reading, even if I want to nap there. They will come down the hill, carrying their backpacks, snack bags, and Cindy with the red wagon full of groceries, swim gear, and fishing bait.

Oh, and did I mention? Cindy is now the official cook. She wisely promoted me to being a fulltime Nana. It is my job to pump water, do dishes, and go swimming with the kids.

I am so grateful!

Ella

Ella Doth, age 14, 2024
Wrote this for a Digital Diary with the prompt:
Where is your happy place?

My happy place is my cabin. It's a place that I have been to a lot and really enjoy it there. It's very secluded. I like to go there to get away. Sometimes I just go up there with a friend of my choice, my grandma, and one of her friends. We call this Girls' Camp. I really enjoy it. It's different from the way I live at home, in the sense that my cabin doesn't have running water, good cell service, and is on a lake. My great-grandpa built it in the woods in Wisconsin. It's roughly a five-plus hour drive to get there. I still really enjoy it and some days I wish I was there instead of at home.

His Words

He gave me the matches
and sent me down the lane.
"Bears are afraid of fire,"
he said.

I set off, a child trusting her father,
never questioning his words nor my safety,
as dusky shadows stretched
between cabins.

I never got to light my matches,
see the bear, nor test Dad's wisdom,
but his words sent me confidently over
life's roads.

The Cabin Quilt

First published in *Her Voice*, Spring 2019

*M*om and I spent the morning pumping water into pails, heating the dish water, dipping the breakfast dishes into the suds, then the near boiling rinse before placing them in the rack by the open window. Steam rose off the flat pancake plates, fruit saucers, and coffee mugs. Zen housework.

I surveyed the interior of the cabin that became mine when my father died two summers ago. Since then, Mom and I bought a new sleeper-sofa, removed faded calendar pages of loons from the porch wall, and took down several sets of deer antlers. The latter felt like treason. Even those bright yellow outhouse toilet seat lids he painted with smiley faces were difficult to discard. Maintenance and minor aesthetical changes were emotionally easier.

Like the quilt I found at the neighborhood garage sale where my mother lives. We had just returned from the cabin and wondered about all the cars blocking her street when she remembered: The Annual Block Sale. I edged between parked cars and inattentive pedestrians before reaching her driveway. While I unpacked the car, I noticed all variety of toys and children's shoes just one door down. I am not a shopper, but I do have grandkids and collect shoes for Guatemala.

"Hey, Mom," I yelled out from behind the car. "What do you think of this toddler basketball hoop for James?" Then added, "Wanna help me shop for shoes?" Soon, we had a dozen pair for only $9.50! The buying bug bit and we walked on, in case something else might "call our name." And, there it was.

Alone in the corner, folded nicely and smelling of fresh laundering, a blue and red quilt smiled at me. I pretended not to notice, but found my feet shuffling in its direction. Why would such a beautiful thing be abandoned to a garage sale? Unfolding it, the pattern emerged revealing red hearts, multiple blue squares, and golden edging. I gently ran my fingers over the swirled stitching and asked the owner about its size. "A queen," she responded. "And, the price?" I asked. "Ten dollars."

A voice inside my head screamed, "Only $10 for a quilt? Is this for real? How can you not spend $10 on such a fine piece of work?" Then, its contrary twin chimed in: "You don't need a quilt. What will you do with it?" Followed by: "But, $10 for a queen-sized, hand sewn quilt? You're kidding. Buy it!"

"What is the story behind this quilt?" I asked, hoping to block out my mind chatter.

"It was left here when we moved in last year. There is a patch inside with the name of the lady who made it. That's all we know."

I checked for the patch. Oh, my. Ashley and Dan, June 18, 2011, Made by Grandma Lian. That was only four years ago. Have they divorced already? But, wouldn't you keep something Grandma made even if you didn't keep the spouse? Was this quilt unlucky? Impossible. It was made by a grandma.

Clearly, it needed to be loved. It would go to the cabin. It could go in the guest bedroom and that bedspread and curtains could be bumped into the loft. Then, that bedspread would move to... well, I'd figure out something. For sure, I'd have to find different curtains to match.

Next trip north, I stopped at The Cabin Store's sale corner and, for 50% off, discovered laced valences patterned with pine branches and pine cones. Not the cheery red or blue curtains I had envisioned, but why not airy cream-colored valences? Two for the price of one, only $20. No more head debates.

Before lunch, I snuck in and hung them without Mom noticing. After the quilt and valences were in place, I called her out of the kitchen and into the side bedroom. With a flourish and a 'ta-da,' I opened the door and let her in.

"Oh, it is perfect!" she exclaimed. "The color, the light, it is so perfect!" Then, we both looked down at the orange shag throw rug and simultaneously said, "That will have to go."

The family arrives tomorrow. The water pails are full and the orange rug replaced by a new blue rag rug Mom found at a craft fair. The little brown Styrofoam owls still cling to their plastic perch over the corner clothes rack, but we'll deal with them another day.

Red Barn Dishes
Greg wonders... Why?

August 1, 2020:

*G*reg arrived and began the downsizing quest. He brought with him the desire to rearrange, to evacuate the unused, and to lighten the load, following the passing of his Grandpa Don, the cabin's patriarch. The following was our basic exchange as we sorted through each room:

"What about all of these games on the bookshelf?" he asked me, pointing to an overflow.

"Good place to start. Which games do you think you and the kids would play and take the rest."

He gathered the rejects into a corner for the Goodwill store and scanned the area for another spot for the keepers.

"What's in the buffet?" he asked on his way over to open the doors. Behind the first door, Mom stored her very favorite dishes from the 1950s, the Red Barn collection.

"Are these dishes important?" Greg queried. He took them out one by one and placed them on the table for review. "Look, this is all old chipped china!"

"Yes, but..." I trailed off. How was I going to explain the heart strings pulling at my childhood memories of all the meals she served on them? They were yellow, with green trim, a cherry tree and a red barn, so very colorful and artistic. "No, not yet," I whimpered. "But," in a gesture toward compromise, "Let's get them out and put them in a box while I think about it."

After carefully packing them away, he filled the now empty space with the remaining games and turned his attention to the living room area.

"Why not move the sofa to someplace new?" a seemingly simple request. "Why not put it over here by that wall?"

"Because," I said, not wanting to sound contrary, "Because, if it were there, then people would be facing a wall, not the lake."

"But then," he continued his line of thinking, "you could put the T.V. over in that corner."

"Hm," I pointed out, "the antennae would have to be rerouted upstairs, a hole be cut for the wiring to come through the ceiling..."

"And then," he continued without taking in the gravity of my domino effects theory, "the T.V. would be so much easier to see over there. This space would allow for a much larger screen and we wouldn't have to move all the chairs to face it."

These points were all true, but overlooked the fact that the television was not, is not, nor ever will be the focal point of my lifestyle, unlike the 54-some-inch T.V. at his house, poised so that people eating in the kitchen can watch it!

Leaving that detail out of the discussion, I put it this way, "We bought that T.V. for your grandmother so she can feed her news habit. From that recliner chair, she can do her crosswords on the flip down desk, put her coffee on the side table, and is close to the T.V. without the rest of us having to listen."

My father passed away in 2013, leaving my mother, now aged 94, as the matriarch. She wasn't here today due to her concern about COVID. Perhaps her absence would enhance our often heart-rendering task of sorting through habits and our collective stuff. Or not.

"Greg," I looked at him and shook my head, "your ideas are valid and appreciated. I probably sound contrary, but it is about logistics. Your Grandpa put in the electric here and the outlets are all on one side. City codes weren't a thing then, so regularly positioned outlets didn't happen. The porch wall is single-boarded, impossible to string wires, leaving long extension cords dangling everywhere. Take a look at the rafters. The lights all have extension cords."

Before going further, we decided it would be beneficial to do a complete walk through. We looked at the brown 4 by 8 foot wall paneling in each bedroom with remnants of 1960s green shag rugs, recycled from the Eau Claire living room, covering the floors. We pulled open dresser drawers, kitchen cupboards, and perused the wall decorations, many calendar pages of loons hanging by two tacks. We read the cartoons stuck to the fridge forever.

This place was built by my father, Donald, and his father, Floyd in 1957. My mother, Phyllis, had added her feminine and artistic touches over the decades, including the Red Barn dishes, also recycled from the Eau Claire home. Now, with the pandemic, would she ever leave there and return to the cabin?

In case she does, I can't get rid of her favorite Red Barn Dishes...

Not just yet.

Addendum:

On September 11, 2020, my mother was having trouble breathing. The doctor's appointment revealed a lung full of fluids — Pleural Effusion. She left the office with a DNR (Do Not Resuscitate) bracelet and signed forms for hospice. She died on November 14, 2020.

The following summer, Greg and I continued our quest. Among other things, I painted the brown paneling cream, took out the shag rugs, brought up my grandma Nellie's spindle bed, and yes, we donated the box of Red Barn dishes to Goodwill.

My only regret? That mom didn't get to see all of the improvements!

Reflections

Las Sobras

First published in *Her Voice*, July 2021

L as Sobras is the name we finally settled on for the family cabin. Loon-n-Tick was already taken, as was my second favorite, Ne'er Dun.

With the passing of both of my parents, it came time to review the contents of "Las Sobras" and make decisions with the next generation: my son, Greg. Note that Greg will not be taking on this cabin when I am no longer able to. Meanwhile, I review and reflect on next steps. This is where we are now.

I am now in the precarious stage of life called, *La Tercera Edad*, Spanish for "Third Age." I am the only survivor of my immediate family and their preceding generation. I now own my family's cabin. This is my first spring opener alone. Dad taught me about all the locks, which gas for the mower, how to light the stove, and set me up with help for the dock. However, walking into the cabin as a first-time orphan hit hard.

The entry room released a familiar scent of everything inside. I lifted the window blinds and watched two geese swim around the bend of the east bay. Sun shone over the tablecloth Mom fashioned from left over curtains. In the coming days, I would switch out the old green, white trimmed dishes for Mom's everyday set and box them for the Honduran asylum family. I'd cull out sheets and towels. I'd paint the brown paneling a cream color. I would have the urge to call her, a daily habit I had before she died last fall. I even caught myself going for the phone, before stopping and feeling that pang in my heart.

Then, my son arrived to help.

"What is this for? Do you use it? Do we need that?" he began.

"Yes, I use that desk. It was your grandfather's from college."

"And, these four embroidered wall pieces of the chipmunk, squirrel, raccoon, and bunny?"

"Those were done by your great-grandma, Edith. Ever notice all the embroidered pillow cases? All hers."

"How about the embroidery by the sink?"

"Oh, I did those decades ago. Like them?" I winked.

And, so it went. I hadn't realized the family lore had stopped with me.

"The boathouse was once our garage on Rudolph Road," I launched into a story. "Grandpa took it apart a piece at a time, labeled them and reconstructed it up here."

"How about the table on the porch? It takes up a lot of room."

"Grandpa found it at his rental place. Refinished it. I prefer eating out there."

"Look!" I heard him yell out, "Under their bed!"

I got to the door as my son held up, or should I say down, two shotguns.

"Whew," I breathed relieved. "I thought you found something dead!"

By day's end, he learned that the wood box had once been Grandpa's baby bed, the yellow dishes with the barn and cherry tree pattern were Grandma's favorite, the rag rugs were from 1940s pant scraps, like the quilt he has at home from Great-grandma Nellie.

Leftovers. Sobras. Recycled. Repurposed. Re-imagined. A family that handed down their Great Depression habits — all remarkable. But now what?

"Should we sell and buy a place closer?" he ventured. "This is a seven-hour drive. It doesn't even have indoor plumbing!"

The evening lake stilled. The two geese screeched into takeoff. The spring peepers were delightfully deafening. A soft rain tapped on the roof. We were tired and hungry.

"What should we have for supper?" he asks.

"Leftovers," I respond. "Let's use the leftovers."

Phyllis planted some forget-me-nots that rarely bloomed, until the summer after she died. They came up everywhere.

Steven Darrell Kurtz

April 10, 1955 — December 5, 1985
My Brother

*A*pril 10, 1955 was a Sunday. My father was preaching and my mother was giving birth to Steven. I was two-and-a-half years old and don't remember where I was! Pictures show me holding this tiny, new addition to my world. Pictures are the only evidence I have of our activities until we moved to Three Lakes the year my dad took leave of the church to build our cabin.

They found a rental house in Three Lakes, a few blocks from the school, two blocks from the Post Office, and about three from Dobb's General Store, depending if you took the sidewalk or went through the empty lot. Stevie and I got our own rooms upstairs along with a room used for storage by the owner. It was "verboten" to enter, as her worldly goods were stored there. It was a jungle of piled up possessions. How do I know? We snuck in. Today, this house is the Historical Museum.

Mom recalls her winter there as bleak, snow-filled, lacking social life, especially for women, and a coal-filled furnace that barely kept us from freezing. We attended services at the United Church of Christ, a quaint, white, steepled building with lovely stained glass windows and a woman pastor, Rev. Margaret Beck. Each Sunday, the service began with the hymn, Holy, Holy, Holy.

Dad took a job with Cy Williams, a famous baseball player turned architect/builder. Perhaps Dad's experience there helped him with the cabin construction. That is, until the day Cy's place burned down. Dad tells of picking up his lunch pail and going to his friend, John Cooley, in the Forest Service. He was hired the same day to hunt porcupine and "disappear" unused equipment, so that new could be purchased, an unsavory job for his character.

Mom stayed home with Stevie and I was sent to the first grade at age four, because there was no kindergarten. We ice skated in the lot next door, now a library, walked to the original Post Office for our mail, and bought penny candy at Dobb's, where they still made change by sending bills to the upstairs loft-balcony overlooking the main floor in a container with a pulley system — such is my recall. Stevie and I played with a few friends from school and nearby. By second grade, Dad took a job at First Congregational Church in Eau Claire and we moved.

Again, there were two bedrooms upstairs and we each got one. His was the warm one. I was given a space heater. I got the double bed, he got the twins. I got pink walls, bedspread, and curtains. Hot pink. He got subtle earth tones — or was that later? Our lives were divided by the hallway. He collected rocks, butterflies, shells, and books that identified them. I played Barbie. We both played Red Rover, Kick Ball, Come to see the Ghost Tonight, to name a few, with a flock of friends provided by the neighborhood, Catholic families mostly, numbering ten to twelve kids each. The lawns were mowed, vegetable and flower gardens flourished, and sidewalks were straight. We walked to school and rode bikes.

I guess, if someone painted a picture of that period of our lives, it would have a touch of Norman Rockwell. By 14, he was given special permission to work at Michelle's pet shop. He dyed my pet poodle, Mimi, blue for Easter. He was a school patroller and that year won a trip to Washington, D.C., for his service. Steven earned an A in every one of his classes — in my opinion without even trying. He played piano, viola, a variety of wooden recorders, and his masterpiece, the oboe. Each new instrument brought unfamiliar screeches into the house until he mastered them. His time was divided between biking with Randy Burss to their "Daphnia" pond in search of all living things found floating there and other hours spent with musical practices, concerts, and contests.

But paintings are one dimensional. I'm not really sure how easy life was for Steven. After I left for college, he "came out" to our parents. I was not there and only heard about the conversation years later. This was in the 1970s. What was his life really like in a homophobic world? Mothers were blamed for the "tendencies" of gay sons. A good friend of mine asked me if I still loved him. Really? Oh, my god. You have to be kidding! What did Steven endure?

Next there was AIDS. Steven was living in Chicago with his partner, George, when he was diagnosed. Mom rushed to clean and sanitize everything so that her son would not contract any other illness that would exacerbate his decline. I joined her. Misinformation, fear, and grief ran rampant. Six months later, Steven was sent to the hospital, again. I was to fly down, but a winter weather threat canceled that. My parents gave permission to stop heroic treatment and left George alone to say his goodbyes.

Steven's death devastated Mom and Dad. I was numbed and converted into an only child. I continue to think of what it would be like to still have him here. He missed Greg's growing up, and never met Greg's kids. These are melancholy thoughts of loss to us all. I write to process. I write to share, to keep my loved ones alive. With that, I give you Steven, a handsome, talented, funny guy who bears remembering!

Cabin circa 1961-62

Reading to Greg, 1981-82

Steven, the musician, playing Grandma Nellie's pump organ
and his latest instrument, the viola, at age 10

Our former home turned into a museum

James Richard Doth
March 31, 1952 — May 23, 1978
In Memory of my first husband and Greg's dad

I met Jim at the ATU house on the Hamline campus in 1972. We were both renting rooms there over the summer. That fall, I left to study in Spain and he was waiting when I returned. The following fall, he came bounding up the stairs to my dorm room and presented me with an engagement ring. I accepted on the grounds that I graduate first and that we go to Spain before any babies. We bought a house in White Bear Lake, Minnesota, were married in Eau Claire, Wisconsin, on September 14, 1974, just three months after my graduation.

Among a multitude of memories are Woody Allen movies, his new, blue, racy Challenger with tape deck blaring Chicago and the Doobie Brothers' tunes, and there was the time he broke into my parent's house through the bathroom window, since they weren't home yet. He bought a speed boat and water skis for summer. He buckled up his boots and skied downhill in the winter. He grilled steaks and drank Whiskey-7. He gardened and pickled his own cucumbers.

If you were sitting at my campfire, under the full moon, watching the lightning bugs blink, we could reminisce for hours about those no longer with us. Saying their names keeps their memories alive. You see, Jim died in a motorcycle accident coming home from his office's softball game in west Minneapolis on the evening of May 23, 1978. I was home with baby Greg, packing to go to the cabin the next morning. Instead, two policemen came to the door, then some of Jim's realtor colleagues, and then, family members. Jim was 25.

Jim the hunter, fsherman, hiker, liked the cabin for all its outdoor opportunities. As a new realtor, he suggested my dad sell it. "It would bring in good money. It's unique, a gem."

Instead, Dad sent us over by the creek to search for morels. Our first time out, we filled the bowl, biting me with the morel bug. I've never since found more than half a dozen, yet I'll never tell you exactly where they were all those decades ago.

Jim and Dad enjoyed putting a worm on the hook or casting off the dock. Under the dock is a notorious spot for panfish, mostly my pets! I feed them bread crumbs when Dad isn't using them in a minnow net. It isn't fair to the fish, but the kids have fun seeing their bobber go down and are in awe when they pull up a sunny the size of a fifty-cent piece, having put up such a fight. We might have invented catch-and-release, since nothing warranted keeping.

The cabin was our go-to Honeymoon destination. I still haven't figured out when my parents snuck up there to decorate the place. There was white crepe paper draped between rafters with white-paper-fold-out bells dangling from lights. It was strange for me to be in charge of cooking, instead of my mom. As a new bride, I was under the misconception that cooking was in my job description. I even served him. I did not make that a habit!

We canoed, hiked, and took a small plane ride up and over the Chain-of-Lakes with a show-off pilot. He ascended into the clouds, swooped back over the forests and then dipped down to show us our cabin, before returning us to the Three Lakes airport. Me? I had the barf bag firmly in my grasp. There is a picture of us in front of the plane after touchdown. My hand is behind my back. Only I knew about the hidden bag, until now.

Good to his promise, we went to Spain before starting a family. We left in September, 1976, for a three-week swing of my favorite places. We saw a bullfight in Madrid, the buried monarchs in El Escorial, stayed with Antonio and met his wife, Maribel, in Seville, took the ferry to Morocco, where I dropped my passport, retrieved by Clive, thus starting a lifelong friendship with him and his wife, Rita. We climbed into the horse-drawn carriage circling the Parque de Maria Luisa, gazed on the great masters' art in The Prado and lived on tapas. We drank water from the fountain in the Alhambra's Patio de los Leones, hoping the legend of a certain return would be true. I broke out of my "wifey" role and surged ahead as an interpreter of language and culture. Gender expectations were forever changed. Our life was further changed eight months later.

Arriving a month before expected, on May 11, 1977, Gregory Ryan Doth was born. By summer, Gregory was sitting in a basin on the kitchen table getting his first cabin bath, given by his father, who was still in the practicing stages, under the watchful eye of his grandpa Don. This was the second generation to be bathed in the basin and the fourth generation to inhabit the cabin. Jim carried Gregory in a backpack for hiking, dipped his feet into the lake, rocked him in Grandma Nellie's antique rocker and put him to bed in the trundle. It was to be the only time Jim and his son were at the cabin together. By the next summer, my dad was the main man in Gregory's life.

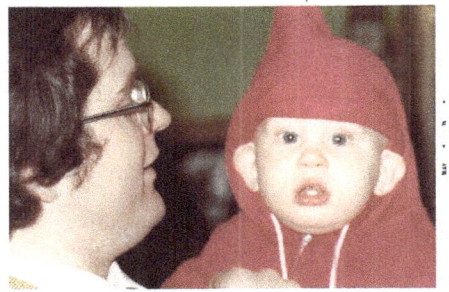

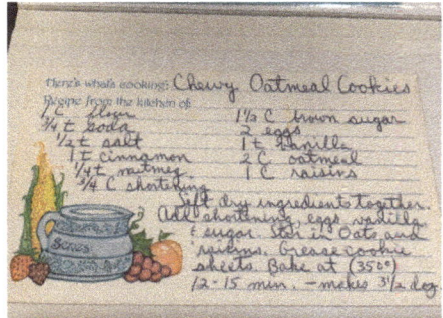

George James Drelles
February 23, 1948 – April 26, 2005
Son of Constantine "Gus" Drelles & Kaliopy (Kepros) Drelles

*S*trange about these things. George came into my life via my brother, Steven. I assume they came together over their love of pitcher plant orchids, tropical fish, talking parrots, classical music, and art. I say assume, because I never asked.

Strange that I never asked George about his family, about his youth, about his lifelong passions. I found some of this out today when I Googled his obituary. This is one of those missed opportunities. He was part of my life for 15 years or so. We sat on the end of the dock at midnight and watched for shooting stars, but I never asked about his boyhood. We had long phone calls, but I never inquired about his parents. We took care of my brother in his last months, but never spoke of our fears.

What I do know is that George revered his Greek heritage. He looked Greek, if there is such a thing. He was slender, tanned, handsome, courteous, funny, but I'm breaking the first commandment of a good writer. I am telling, not showing!

George sent goofy cards. Like the cartoon of people circling bushes with egg beaters that read: No more beating around the bush... followed by a birthday greeting. George always mailed a large box of presents at Christmastime, always, always with Frango chocolates included. It was his trademark.

His gifts to Greg were innovative, technological, hands-on. It didn't matter that Greg might have been too young for these contraptions, but they were forward thinking, a challenge to send him beyond plastic toys. He wanted to be Uncle George, even more so after Steven died.

What to do with George after Steven was gone? There were no legal tie options for them at the time. Gay marriage wouldn't be legal for decades. In the absence of societal recognition, we simply called him Uncle and he was a chosen part of our family. He and Steven loved going to the cabin. Steven soon introduced him to the Pot Hole, our name for the cove protected from motorboats and staring eyes. The Pot Hole, home to beaver, dragonflies, bullfrogs, and wood ducks. There, they beached their boat and climbed out into the soft, mushy bogs in search of the pitcher plant orchid domain. It was there they wanted their ashes sprinkled. Only Steven got his wish.

George knew how to wear a suit, prepare a Greek feast, teach parrots to talk, and put up with boa constrictors in 100-gallon tanks when Steven was called upon to baby sit for the pet shop. He was clean-cut, well-mannered, a regular gentleman. Mom thought him to be perfect husband material, and he was, for Steven. It is worth noting that Mom had a high bar regarding men.

With George, she was able to share her love of wildflowers, compare recipes, listen to Mozart, and laugh at her own foibles. With George, Dad had a fishing companion. With George, Greg had another gamer to play D&D or go tubing to Grass Island. With George, I had another brother after Steven died and left us to tell the stories. Would that they could be around my cabin campfire now, answering the questions I neglected to ask.

Lost by Bailey Lake

October 1990

Diary...Lake Julia...A LOST DAY LOST IN THE WOODS..OR WAS IT?

More than ever before I became aware on this day that one can plan and plan and plan but when _our_ plans are not realized may there be a way to keep from drowning in self pity anger and disappointment. I left the cabin at 8:30 a.m. this day with the intent of going to the ski hill, the location of the old fire tower, Bailey Lake and back home on Lake Julia.. Total distance of 4 miles perhaps....

With a pedometer in place...but no compass!..my walk began with an intent to walk no more than 6 miles and return to the cabin by noon. What actually happened was a "walk" that went at least 17 1/2 miles and lasted 7 1/2 hours. The details of this "lost" experience are not as important at the fact that paths that are numerous (logging trails, snowmobile trails, horseback riding paths and miscellaneous "government roads) are open for choices that can soon confuse ones orientation on a cloudy day and these labyrinths don't connect with where one has wishes to go.

Fortunately for me when I did emerge from the forest on "Back Tracker" road which was graveled and then to a black top known as Hay Meadow Road, a woman riding on a bicycle was of some help. She had come from Seven Mile Lake.

I was quite fatigued. My pedometer indicated that I was about 12-14 miles from home for sure. The pedometer had registered about 18 miles and I had circled and back tracked more than a few times. I asked the lady which way I should continue on Hay Meadow Road to get to Lake Julia. She looked puzzled and said "where is that"? She indicated that she had come from Forest Road 2178 and that helped. After about two miles of walking further a car came by. I "thumbed a ride". At first it looked like the man was going to drive by. I couldn't blame him if he had because I was still carrying my shot gun that I had brought along in the morning with the idea of hunting some partridge (Ruffed Grouse). He stopped in spite of the fact of my being in blue jeans, a hunting jacket, camouflaged cap and shotgun. Thank goodness country people tend to help out one another.

The man was from Butternut Lake and had once owned Blue Echo Resort. He gave me a ride to forest road 2184 which was only 3 miles now from the cabin. He would have taken me home but he had a "deadline" of getting to Crandon to pick up his daughter from work.

On the walk I did not panic. I walked through areas ravaged by fire. Maple sections of forest were brilliantly colored in orange and red. Tall pines darkened many sections on an already heavily overcast sky. Pine squirrels were frolicking everywhere. They chattered greetings AND scholdings. A few wild geese (Canada) had flown over. When I got home about 5 P.M. I drank much water to handle my thirst and when directly to bed for a sound night of deep sleep. My plans weren't realized...but what an experience...missing Bailey Lake ...and wandering into no man's land.

The following morning it was placid and quiet on lake Julia. The morning news revealed a gunman was holding people hostage in a hotel in Berkely, California. The news also featured scripts of broken lives of adult children from broken alcoholic family members as well as U.S. soldiers expressing greetings from Saudi Arabia to their families in the U.S.A.

Copied from Donald Kurtz Journal

Ghost Cabin

*I*f there is no one in the cabin, does it exist? If no one is here to smell the balsam, is it scentless? If there is no one here to listen to the gold finch and the robin, are they mute? If there is no one to feel the warmth of the army blanket, is it useless? If the window is closed and the breeze does not blow the metal owl wind chimes, does their music die?

I am in a ghost world. A ghost cabin in the ghost woods on a ghost lake. I am the only human around. The thunderstorm took away the two fishing boats and the car took away my parents. So, this is what it is like when no one is here.

The cabin structure stands, still full of echoes of this morning's breakfast preparations. The sound of the toast descending into the toaster, the click of the minutes being registered on the microwave, the scrape of the cupboard door as it opened, releasing cereal bowls into my mother's hand. My father's growly voice raising as his spoon clinks against the measuring cup where he stirs his life-giving Citrucel. He is on edge with the leaving, both needing to return to his "other" home for a doctor's appointment, which, by the way, he made, and wanting to stay here in his "heart-home" in the woods. He could have been here a few more days, but the schedule is set and it took them up the hill in a flash of lightning and a clap of thunder. Even now, I wait for a phone call from some wayside rest to assure me of their condition.

Yet, I am allowing myself to sink into the deep of this day, where sounds do not include people's voices. I have wondered how long I could go without human contact. Not that it would be a good idea in the long run, but in short... would I tune in more clearly to the bullfrog, the dragonfly, and the raindrops?

My eyes feast on the pacific lake with its regular ripples and ever changing reflections. The winds have stopped and the subtle breeze barely touches the birch leaves as it moves through. The bull frog has taken up with the purple finches in their song rising from the east bay to my cabin window.

Usually, my head is so full of voices that I do not notice. If I were not here, would that baby chipmunk be enjoying that wild strawberry any less? He circles this morsel of red around and around, savoring it. A piece that I would pop into my mouth and barely notice the squirt of sweet or sour it released. But he sits there, turning it with his tiny paws until it completely disappears and then springs into a leap, bounding over the grasses.

I imagine the eons before humans walked this earth. Like this morning, I expect the tree boughs still dipped in the wind, rocking the robin's nest. The animals scurried about their food collections. The waves came into the shore.

I imagine our lives today... heads bent into the wind, scurrying around on our quest for sustenance, likely headed into the waves and not floating with them. You know the phrase: "going with the flow." Well, are you paying attention to the planet?

It could become a ghost cabin in a ghost woods. How long would those hats hang there until nature reclaimed this porch, that water dipper, those china lovebirds? Will the strawberries be here next spring for that chipmunk?

Snippets

Time

Oh, calendar! With your
blessed chunks of time
all caged into neat
squares in which we
number our escaping days.

Oh, ticking clock! Whose
hands direct the traffic of
our minutes and hours
herding us along a highway
of maintenance and meetings.

Oh, to live by the inner nudges!
Sunlight waking us, hunger leading
us to the table and weariness
shutting our eyelids at the end
of a job gratefully done.

Oh, Life! Parade us gently
over your timeline, minus
the panicked blur of flipping
calendar pages, into a flow
of sunrises and sunsets.

The Truth Behind Nature Poems

First published in *Her Voice*, Summer 2023

How does a poem come to be?
Start with the leaning white pine tree?
Bonsai bent away from the prevailing
westerly winds my canoe is tailing?

I could add a rabbit up on that hill
with an eagle above it, nesting still.
Or, the three otter noisily skimming
the lakeshore, busily trimming...

The white lily flowers for munching
in their late afternoon lunching.
While the great blue heron is stalking
the bullfrogs that are busily talking.

Would a woodland poem mention
the black flies and their intention
to roost on my bare legs and make
snacks of all that they find on the lake?

Or, the evening mosquitoes arriving,
noting it is time to start diving
on us, the warm-blooded creatures
that the woodland, at this hour, features!

The dragonfly now takes his cue
and sweeps in for the mosquito,
but didn't take into account the bass
breaking the waves with one strong pass.

Yes, the woodland can be serene,
but looking past the tranquil scene,
one might note the natural pain,
for we are all part of... the food chain!

Destination Hammock

Published in *The Talking Stick,* vol. 33, 2024
Jackpine Writers' Bloc Inc. Menahga, MN

The hammock stretches out
between two trees on the shoreline.

Up at the cabin, I begin to pack
for my trip down the hill,

where the sun-sparkled waves and
lake scented breeze whisper,

teasing me through the open window.
I pull on my swim suit and get my beach bag.

I'll need sunscreen, sunglasses, sunhat,
flip-flops; bug spray, towel, water bottle.

Add a book, an art tablet, colored pencils
and a camera – just in case.

What? A gust of wind?
A pitter-patter on the porch roof,

where I stand, listening,
a proverbial pack mule,

laden with my bag of possibles,
headed out for a hammock afternoon.

But, now? What's this?
The sun rays are being washed away...
        By raindrops.

The Sheltered Valley Chair

*H*ello, I'm the Sheltered Valley Ski chair. Back in 1948, Carl O. Marty Jr. and his brother, Bob, opened the most amazing resort in the north woods known as the Northernaire. (It was designed and built by another renown Three Lakes citizen, Cy Williams.) These men offered a destination to those big city people yearning for a "nature" experience. The Chicago and Northwestern Railroad often ran Northernaire specials, bringing the urban tourist to town for the spa, entertainment, skating, and – skiing.

That is where I come in. In the mid-1950s, a meandering journey along Military and Sheltered Valley roads opened onto a chalet, perched on a leveled-off shelf overlooking some of the higher hills in the region. That was the site of the Sheltered Valley Ski Area! Runs were cleared and rope tows added for this all-inclusive ski experience.

The inside was handsomely decorated with wood paneling, a stone fireplace, pegs to park your skis, and a full-service restaurant. I am one of the original chairs used at the Chalet to give the tired skiers a place to settle in. People would move me over to the large windows for a better view of incoming skiers and the woods beyond.

Then, the day came when the Northernaire buses no longer unloaded skiers in the parking lot. The building was closed – vacated – a ghost chalet. Sadly, this was a temptation to adventurers with other sports in mind. Windows were broken, doors were removed, interior decorations and furnishings were vandalized. Some folks found the area perfect for unofficial bonfires and parties. That is where my story of rescue takes place.

Somewhere around 1979, two men from an area cabin, with the purpose of seeing what shape the Chalet was in, hiked over and entered the building. There, among the broken pieces, two chairs, one with yellow tapestry cloth, and me, in my plain ivory covering, sat untouched. When these two guys hoisted us over their heads and bush-wacked their way back to the vintage cabin, I called it a rescue.

Until 2022, my buddy chair and I got to sit around a large braid rug in that cabin living room, providing a comfortable spot for many a conversation. Sometimes, someone would jump up with a pair of binoculars and watch the loons out on the lake. Sometimes, kids would curl up with Grandpa, listening to a story. Sometimes, people sat on the edge of their seats, excitedly gesturing, as they told their most recent big fish story!

Without these stories, I am "just" a chair. Now, you know that my story started decades ago, in an historic Ski Chalet, hunkered down in a "Sheltered Valley" in the Nicolet National Forest. Now that you've heard my story, we are connected. Now, you are part of the history.

2023 Kyle reinacts the recovery of historic material for the Three Lakes Museum.

"After about three visits to the lodge, I took an arm chair and dinner table chair to the cabin before they were all smashed and trashed." (see page 33 for the whole story)

Fun Facts (Not) Forgotten

The Road Commissioner

From the beginning, my father was the unofficial "keeper" of the roadways. His upbringing refused to allow degradation and unsafe passage, despite the stand-offish, disinterested demeanor of his one-time partner and neighbor – Ed. In a 1993 letter welcoming the Frankes, our new neighbors, he described this part of the Kurtz history. Don wrote:

"During the 42-years, Donald learned the practices of being 'road commissioner' from cutting brush back from the banks to permit sun drying the roads, planting sod in washed out ruts, and getting occasional loads of gravel – saved the mufflers of the Kurtz cars and their visitors. Mr. Zager owned a truck of some description most of these years and was not concerned with road conditions, except the less passable they were, the less likely were there to be sightseeing trespassers.

Initially, the road crossed the creek upstream from the present crossing. Beaver continually plugged the culverts. The 'road

commissioner' personally replaced the crossing four times. Once a bulldozer was required for the job. On one occasion, on my arrival, I discovered Edward crossing a ten-foot long and five-foot deep gully with his vehicle... on planks."

In Ed's own words, regarding road repair: "I don't help, because I only use that hill going down."

Saving the Monarchs

It never occurred to me as a child that one day Monarch butterfly existence would be threatened. Over several summers, I noticed fewer and fewer until the news was official. The monarch habitat in Mexico was being cut down and their migratory paths were being destroyed by pesticides and massive ditch mowing, killing milkweed and cocoons.

The milkweed along Sheltered Valley Road produced multiple eggs and caterpillars, which I carted back to the cabin, put into jars with a stick and topped with cheesecloth. Each day, I gathered fresh milkweed and emptied the jars of their leavings until the caterpillar climbed the stick and formed its cocoon. They didn't always hatch within the time of my stay, so I crawled under the front entry stoop and duct taped the sticks below, out of the reach of rain and rodents. On my return, I'd find empty transparent cocoons, cracked open, having let free their miracle monarchs to continue the cycle to Mexico. In 2017, I fulfilled a dream of traveling to the Rosario Monarch Sanctuary in Michoacan, Mexico with my traveling buddy, Jamy O.

Family furnishings

Nellie's Spindle bed and Aunt Edna's Commode

The spindle bed belonged to Nellie Kurtz in Rock Grove. She painted it white and turquoise, which her son, Donald, painstakingly refinished to its present wood stain at this date (2024).

The commode belonged to "Aunt" Edna, a woman who lived beyond a century, piano teacher to generations of youth in Dakota, Illinois. Phyllis refinished the commode to go with the spindle bed. When Dave Goeke visited in 2022, I pointed out embroideries by Edith Wise, the wooden chalice by Glenn Wise, the paintings by Phyllis, before getting to the spindle bed and commode. When I opened the door and read the note left by mom regarding its history, he exclaimed, "Edna was my piano teacher!" It was so satisfying to welcome Dave to a place filled with his family, as well as mine.

Beulah's Doll Cupboard

Phyllis also refinished a chamber pot commode and the small doll cupboard, now storing toilet paper! It once belonged to her sister, Beulah, and was covered in some unidentifiable tar colored finish. Having many furniture refinishing projects behind her, Phyllis, then

89, donned layers of old clothes, picked up a scraper, the paint stripper can, and elbow greased the cupboard for several days in a row without acceptable results. Exasperated but not defeated, we carted it

to a professional in Chippewa Falls and got the job done!

The Boat House Maple Tree

The cabin became mine, on paper, in 2009. Very quickly, I began to see the cabin from a different perspective. No longer the pampered oldest living adult child, floating in my father's kayak and eating my mother's feasts, I was a land owner with responsibilities! That is when I noticed the maple tree that grew up in front of the Boat house... blocking the one door completely! How did that ever slip by my father's watchful eye?

This was no recent maple. Estimated height of 50 feet and breadth of 14 inches across (not around, across!) with shadows reaching over the boat house roof, the lawn, the privy, and woodshed, depending on the time of day. It could have been easily removed for years – nay, decades!

Dad was an expert sawyer, keeping a chainsaw ready for trees blocking roads, roof repair, and road building. Robert was/ is the only chainsaw man to meet his prowess.

The maple removal however, fell to me. I called the Klessig Brothers Tree Service. Four men arrived, a specialist in shinnying up towering trees, a guy in a cherry-picker basket, another driving the chipper, and the last calling out guidance to get through the lane. A few hours later, only a short stump remained, which Robert axed out the following year. Me? I wrote a check for $600 and ever since have kept my eyes on trees growing in places that they shouldn't!

Critters at the Creek: Suckers, Snappers, and Minnows

Our lane ran about a half mile over Nicolet National Forest land before coming to the creek, where Dad erected a "government specified" gate at the bridge, designating the beginning of private property. Furbush Creek was locally known for sucker fishing runs and snapping turtle egg laying in the spring. The locals used to bring their nets and walk into the creek and swoop up their catch, which was usually taken to old refrigerators or other contraptions, for smoking. You know, smoked fish!

Far less popular were the snapping turtles, often of notable size – think bushel basket. I do not know how they hauled themselves up Dad's rock wall embankment, but they loved the looser gravel and sunshine found on the culvert bridge. To my knowledge, only Ed's dad, Herbert Zager, hunted the turtles, taking them back to his wife, Alma, to turn them into soup.

The rest of us experienced the large snappers as road blocks. There was no driving around them when laying eggs – a prolonged process. Memories of my dad finding a limb and placing it by the turtles strong, snapping snout usually did the trick. Their reaction

was to clamp on, at which time he would lift them up and out of the way. Note, these turtles can do you damage!

The bridge was also the site of minnow trapping. We took the traps with bread crumbs, tied them to a sumac growing there, and threw them into the bubbling water. In later years, we began to support Jok'in Joe's Bait and Tackle, in town. Jok'in Joe really did tell jokes. The one I heard the most involved a man of few domestic talents around his bachelor pad. When asked how he washed his dishes, the man replied, "With soap and water," then he put his plate on the floor, went to the door and yelled out, "Here, Soap, Come, Water. Get on in here!" and two hounds came bounding in. For the record, Jok'in Joe's dog was named: Potlicker.

Porcupines in the Pines

On that summer's day, Mom prepared her usual tasty, light lunch and had called Dad and me to the porch table, overlooking the lake. We held hands and Dad said a prayer. For years, this was our ritual, Mom on one end, Dad on the other, and me in the middle, facing the lake. The windows were cranked open and lake breezes came in with sounds of squirrels, yellow finches and... what was that? Dad was in his 80s, but his hunter hearing was alert. Without a clue, he pushed himself away from the table, went into the cabin and returned with his shotgun. This man had hunted, trapped, and fished all his life, but this was lunchtime, it wasn't hunting season for anything we knew of and, he was, after all, in his 80s!

He attempted to be quiet as he opened the screechy screen door, went down the steps, around the west side of the cabin and... Bam! We heard a shot. Then, BAM! We heard another one.

Then quiet. Mom and I looked at each other wide-eyed, then scooched our chairs back and headed outdoors, just in time to see him lay out two porcupines on the lawn. He grinned at us and reported, "These two aren't going to eat any more of our pines now," and he went back inside to finish his lunch.

Towns Folk

Marian Ruth West

From obituary by Smith West Chapel, Billings, MT

"Marian Ruth West, 102, of Billings moved peacefully to heaven on October 17, 2022. She was born July 21, 1920 to Cy and Vada Williams. She was the second youngest of 2 brothers and 1 sister. She grew up with her family on a farm but her father was often absent as he played baseball for the Chicago Cubs and Philadelphia Phillies. Marian always loved the fame of her dad. Marian graduated from Three Lakes High School. She met her husband dealing cards at the Showboat. He lost money but gained a wife. She loved cards her whole life and was a good player. When she counted for her teacher in first grade it was 1, 2, 3, 4, 5, 6, 7, 8, 9, 10, Jack, Queen, King."

I first met Marian at the First Congregational Church, UCC in Three Lakes. She and husband, Cliff, were good friends of my parents. At one time, she had a gift shop outside of town on the way to Eagle River. I was quite young and remembered being amazed at "all the stuff" she had there. My friendship began with her around the 1990s when I began enjoying the Women's Church Bazaar. Each woman busily produced their crafts or baked goods to raise money for a collection of mission work they sponsored. The church basement was filled with decorative tables, inexpensive gifts to family treasures, and their clever creations. I was particularly drawn to Marian's embroidered sayings made into refrigerator magnets. Her choices reveal a sense of humor and feminist flare. I bought one of each!

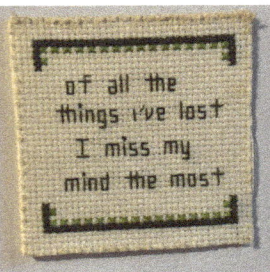

At some point, perhaps n her 80s, she moved to be closer to her family in Montana. It was then we became pen pals. She always painted a cardinal or other nature scene on her notes until she was no longer able to write. One of her favorite stories, that even made it into the Three Lakes paper, told of the time she was treed by a bear!

Mandy and Paul

The cabin company left, so Mom and I pulled off all the sheets, collected the dirty beach towels and filled two laundry baskets for our trip to town. Usually, Mom hauled all of these items back to Eau Claire where she washed, dried, and ironed everything before the return trip north. Perhaps it was because I was along to help that we added "do laundry" to our chore list.

Since Mom rarely did the wash in town, she might have missed this tidbit, but that day, Mom came running back out to the car and burst out, "The woman in there, the owner, she speaks Spanish!" She drug me back into the building and plopped me in front of a small, blond woman who greeted me with, "Hello, sweetie!" Something I later learned she said to everybody.

I returned her greeting, but in Spanish, and we were off! "Ay, Sweetie, me llamo Mandy y este es mi esposo, Pablo. Bueno, Paul, pero mejor Pablo." Her pronunciation came out, "Me jamo" and I guessed Argentinian. Yes, she was from Argentina, but her husband was from the United States. At some point, they landed in Three Lakes and opened up the Laundromat across from the gas station. This was our first day of a long friendship formed through a ritual over laundry. This is the basic translation, with sweetie interjected lavishly thoughout.

"Hola sweetie, come back here to the big washer. Looks like you have some bedding."

"Just put a half cup detergent in. Don't want it to bubble over."

"Here, let me take that. You really need to use the extractor, Sweetie. Save you on the dryer."

"I've got a quarter to put in," she always said as she took the wet clothes out of my hands, circled them around the extractor basin and tucked the towel over everything before closing the lid. How did she make any money?

Between loading machines from the incoming resort patrons, we'd carry on our Spanish conversations. She told me about her visits to her mom back home. What is it like living here? How was her mom? How was my mom? "Sweetie" punctuated every story, sad, bad, or glad.

On the way out the door, she'd tuck a Jehovah's Witness AWAKE magazine on top of the folded clothes. "Sweetie, the Lord loves you. Maybe there's something in here for you."

And then, one summer, she was walking slowly. She leaned in and whispered, "Sweetie, I'm not well. Losing my energy. Trying to figure this out." And, the next summer, she was gone.

Paul carries on. We still speak in Spanish. He keeps this photo of Mandy on the wall. Now, he gives me a quarter for the extractor and tells me to use the bottom dryer.

Three Lakes Flea Market

From Memorial Day to Labor Day, Three Lakes is the site of a Flea Market in Cy Williams Park on Wednesdays. There are, or at least were, antiques, handicrafts, agates, vintage games and records, birch bark baskets, nature photos, and paintings by local artists. My favorite stop was the table in front of the truck selling Amish jams and jellies. All things Amish have the reputation of being delicious, but that is not what brought me to this annual ritual.

Over ten years ago, my parents and I stopped during our in-town chores to just browse around. We all went separate ways, poking at things, noticing antiques that we had used in our own lifetimes, scoped out what prices these items were bringing and then, I heard it. Spanish.

I didn't know that I needed a large jar of Bumbleberry jelly until I got closer. Yes, they were speaking Spanish to each other and then the man turned to a customer and, in English, began running down his menu — blueberry, rhubarb, blackberry, peach, strawberry, all in jams or jellies, some seedless. I waited. When it came my turn, I blurted out a greeting in Spanish and got a wall-to-wall grin, before he called his wife over. That is the way I met Ricardo and Maria.

Every summer, we greet each other like long lost friends, despite taking years of short visits at their table to roll out our mutual stories. Ricardo jokes about being the younger man, about six months maybe, to his wife, now both in their 90s. Every summer, I wonder if they will be there, so I can buy up the small jars for Christmas gifts and sit under the shade of their tent.

The past few years, they've been joined by Maggie and Carolina, two adult daughters who come in for a stint of living in the Northwoods. You see, Ricardo and Maria have a route. There is a Flea Market somewhere every day of the week. It has been such a pleasure and a joy to reunite with these fun-loving, adventuresome elders and their fortunate daughters! Gracias, guys!

Union Congregational Church United Church of Christ

My family and I attended this UCC church every summer since 1957. Rev. Margaret Beck was pastor, a woman in a tiny town in the 1950s, no less! In 2018, the congregation celebrated its 100th Anniversary. The bulletin names people who either were or are family friends. Many congregants have now celebrated 90th birthdays or reached 100! Vi Kveck (now in Chicago), Marion West (daughter of Cy Williams and now in Montana), and June McDuffy (long-time organist and choir director, pictured here with the congregation on August 25, 2024) are three long-time members who moved away to be closer to their 70+ aged children! As with many churches today, Union is planning events to attract new membership.

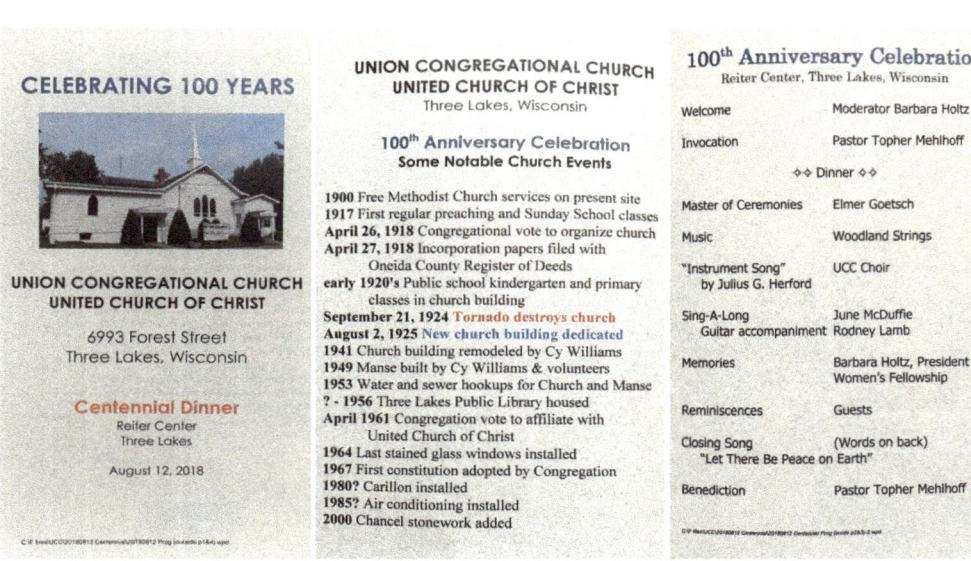

CELEBRATING 100 YEARS

UNION CONGREGATIONAL CHURCH
UNITED CHURCH OF CHRIST

6993 Forest Street
Three Lakes, Wisconsin

Centennial Dinner
Reiter Center
Three Lakes

August 12, 2018

**UNION CONGREGATIONAL CHURCH
UNITED CHURCH OF CHRIST**
Three Lakes, Wisconsin

**100th Anniversary Celebration
Some Notable Church Events**

1900 Free Methodist Church services on present site
1917 First regular preaching and Sunday School classes
April 26, 1918 Congregational vote to organize church
April 27, 1918 Incorporation papers filed with Oneida County Register of Deeds
early 1920's Public school kindergarten and primary classes in church building
September 21, 1924 Tornado destroys church
August 2, 1925 New church building dedicated
1941 Church building remodeled by Cy Williams
1949 Manse built by Cy Williams & volunteers
1953 Water and sewer hookups for Church and Manse
? - 1956 Three Lakes Public Library housed
April 1961 Congregation vote to affiliate with United Church of Christ
1964 Last stained glass windows installed
1967 First constitution adopted by Congregation
1980? Carillon installed
1985? Air conditioning installed
2000 Chancel stonework added

100th Anniversary Celebration
Reiter Center, Three Lakes, Wisconsin

Welcome	Moderator Barbara Holtz
Invocation	Pastor Topher Mehlhoff
◇◇ Dinner ◇◇	
Master of Ceremonies	Elmer Goetsch
Music	Woodland Strings
"Instrument Song" by Julius G. Herford	UCC Choir
Sing-A-Long Guitar accompaniment	June McDuffie Rodney Lamb
Memories	Barbara Holtz, President Women's Fellowship
Reminiscences	Guests
Closing Song "Let There Be Peace on Earth"	(Words on back)
Benediction	Pastor Topher Mehlhoff

Two Famous Locals...

Skip Wagner

Skip Wagner, Mom's favorite entertainer from Showboat fame of playing two trumpets at the same time, died 2023.

Skip Wagner painted this mural in downtown Three Lakes at the Black Forest Bar & Grill.

Fred "Cy" Williams

My dad, Donald, worked for **Cy Williams** during the time our cabin was being constructed, 1957.

Come Sit with Me

Come Sit with Me, My Child

I would like to sit here with you one evening, dear child. We would watch the late afternoon slip into early evening.

The pontoons would take their nightly spin to the end of the lake to watch for wildlife, having already scared any animals off with their motors and loud laughter.

When they leave, a fisherman or two will troll by quietly, with their lure slapping against the water and whir as they reel their lines back in.

When they have tired of casting, the lake begins to look like little raindrops are falling, little circles rippling out. Fish kisses. Bugs come in close and fish surface to take a smacking gulp.

It gets cooler on our skin. Bull frogs start a chorus around the lakeshore. The hummingbirds have left and, if we stay out until dark, there will be lightning bugs.

The western sky is pinkish. The shadows have crawled up the eastern pines and the sun sinks.

Would you come and sit with me, together in this sacred moment of the universe?

Evening on the Shore

*H*ow did this happen? The passing of time, and I'm still sitting in this place, looking out over the lake as if it is the first time. A bee buzzes. Air flows through the mallard's wings, lifting off the water. Circle ringlets spread back into the mirrored surface after the fish caught its fly and gently submerges back below the forest reflections.

It is July. The grasses along the bank are tall, the way my father liked them. "It is an ecological habit," he explained. "Having a grass buffer before the rains run off into the lake is a filter." It also allows for some Joe-Pye weed and daisies to rim the rock wall holding back the erosion, something else he monitors.

In his lifetime, that man, my father, lifted tons of rocks and placed them in layers, holding the esker in a series of terraces, keeping our cabin, the path, the boathouse, and now the swing, in place. When he, his father, his brother, and a raft of friends brought in the horses and bulldozers to literally carve out a spot, he had dreams, a strong back, and an annual wage of less than $3,000. If his dad hadn't floated him a $1,000 loan and lent him the truck to haul some necessities out of Illinois and into this Northwoods, well — as they say — we wouldn't be here.

I never did the math before, but he was 27 when he and his college buddy pooled their reserves and paid $3,500 for 51 acres of north country property, including a long piece of shoreline curving around the peninsula — referred to as The Point. They bought it from one of their university professors, Dr. Harr, who had purchased it from another professor, Dr. Koten, who came by it via a railroad deal. The records do not show any sign of Native Americans, just a sale by the U.S. government dating to Civil War times. That piece of history would be worth researching.

On this tranquil evening of evenings, I am the recipient of all the dreams, labor, road work, black flies, and yes, rock hauling. On this evening, my father's ashes are scattered amongst the retaining walls and over by the yellow shoreline lilies. Some of my mother's ashes grace the flower beds to the east and west of the cabin. Each spring, she and the weeds would return for their annual contest. In the end, they won and now I weed.

Dad's college buddy also stays on the scene from his resting place on the island. I believe my brother finally got his last wish to be scattered among the bog's pitcher plants. His partner wanted to join him, but his family didn't respond to my offer. That leaves me, here on the swing, watching the eternal clouds surface over the western esker, surprising us from behind. Hours have been spent watching them appear, calling out their shapes, and watching them shape-shift, mirrored on the glassy lake below.

Sometimes, we'd have a small bonfire, breaking up twigs to send smoke into the night sky, coaxing the moon to rise and send its path across the lake to where we whispered. How well we knew that the lake didn't keep secrets, as many fishermen's stories came clearly across the waves to our listening ears.

Sometimes, we would throw in an old candle and call out the name of one of our dearly departed, sending love in vapors to them, supposedly, in heaven. Heaven was actually right here. Nearly every time we'd sit here, Dad would say, "This is my little piece of heaven," and we all agreed. The idea of heaven being pearly gates and golden streets made us cringe. Give us this soft green grass for our feet, chipmunk chirping and vireo songs for our listening, and warm breezes upon our skin. We'd look at what seemed to be contiguous grass, only to discover myriad species of wild flowers, clovers, and what the golf course would cover with herbicides.

A whizzing sound and a plunk... a fisherman casts into the lily pads. Tiny grandkid voices wonder about what he will catch. Grandma reminds them to sit down. "Shhh," she says, "don't want to scare the fish."

Another generation learns about worms. "If I were a fish, I'd want a nightcrawler," one little voice says as Grandpa slips one onto a hook. "Grandpa, I got weeds," says the one called Abigail.

"Oh, no, it got off," says Liam. "Watch out for Grandpa's head," Grandma cautions. "Is this a perch?" says the third. Grandma gasps, "Watch out – you snagged Grandpa's shirt!" Grandpa chuckles.

This is what I want for the lake. This is what I hope for the children. This is what I want them to remember when they grow up.

A bull frog starts the nightly roll-call. Another answers. Then another. A half moon is rising.

Grandpa holds up the latest catch and announces, "You have just won the prize for the world's smallest fish!" They cheer, wash their hands in the lake and the motor purrs. "Hold on!" they all yell, as Grandpa revves the speed and careens around Grass Island, sending waves crashing on both shores.

The lake goes back to a mirrored reflection of the shoreline forests. All the clouds have cleared.

I wonder if I'm crazy to be here. Crazy to paint the boathouse shelf, plant more bee balm, and sweep the porch. Am I crazy to sit here letting dusk fall around me, revealing the evening stars? What will I see, what will I hear, what will I remember of past evenings if I stay out here until dark?

I think I'd be crazy not to find out.

Time is Slipping Away

When the skies turned darker, Mom went inside the cabin to check the T.V. for a weather report. Instead, as she adjusted the rabbit ear antenna, a second channel appeared! Something called COZY TV was scrolling through the evening's offerings — a marathon of 1980s comedies — a proverbial time capsule of last century's classics. She turned down the volume on the canned laughter when she heard Dad give out a howl.

A wasp had bitten his finger. His hand was swelling up. He blankly stared at it, void of ability to remember the remedy. He remained immobile while I fetched ice cubes.

Dad moves to the front of the T.V. She tries to see around him. The western sky lightens as the storm rumbles eastward. The clock is headed toward 8:00 p.m. He is headed toward bed. He hangs his white undershirt from the rafters over the woodstove. He shuffles toward his room, past the T.V. advertising an assisted living complex in Merrill.

"All your wants are taken care of," the T.V. announcer gaily chirps. "From cooking to transportation to your medical appointments," he continues, as the camera sweeps over the manicured grounds and into the communal dining room. How soon might that become a necessity for him?

"That storm took away some of our heat!" Mom reports from the recliner she has taken over in his absence. "It's getting cool in here."

Dad turns around and pauses. "Do you want your chair back?" she inquires when he resumes his pacing.

"No, I didn't want it last time and I do not want it now," he spits out on his way to the corner rocker, where he promptly falls asleep, chin on his chest.

Will she get used to his new behaviors? Must she? Is it required?

The sit-com ends, taking with it any residual chuckles. She pushes her head back and pulls the lever to extend the recliner's foot rest. She is so relieved not to have to react or respond. No need to make any more decisions today. The dishes dry in the sink. The sky shifts to the dark of night. There is no reason to consider rallying at this moment.

We descend into the abyss of vintage T.V. shows, sucking us back through decades of by-gone clothing, cars, hairdos, and, compared to the present, mild, almost innocent humor. The T.V. screen flickers in the darkening room, replaying images from the past in a never-ending loop of reruns. Is that what is going on in my father's head? Where is he on the timeline?

Mom and I look up to see a very young Johnny Carson leap onto the stage of his nighttime show after being introduced with Ed McMahon's long, "And, heeeeeeere's Johnny!" Their first guest is the newly discovered Steve Martin.

For a few hours, Mom and I join in the oblivion of time warps, knowing that time is slipping away, and so is he.

The Rememberer

I am a Rememberer. I wonder how many of us are left. In the early origins of humanity, there was no writing. I imagine that, one night while staring into a fire, sounds morphed into language and thereafter, oral traditions evolved.

Just last night, I sat around a fire ring outside a small town library for the purpose of story-telling. The fire was lit, the benches pulled in close, and the sacred food, ingredients in a zip-lock bag for individual serving of s'mores, were lined up next to long, sharp, bamboo shish-kabob sticks. I am now among those the Native Americans reverently call Elders.

I am a Rememberer, the new family elder. That is my chronological place since my mother died. I sense a desire to keep her and the family history alive through stories. My son and his family sit around campfires outside of their pop-up trailer in State Parks, but mostly for the purpose of charring hot dogs, and keeping the mosquitoes at bay.

I am a Rememberer, sitting along the shore of a lake my father came to in the 1950s. So young, so full of dreams, so confident of his muscles and his abilities as fisherman, hunter, father, husband, and preacher. His letters have recently been rediscovered among the treasures of the Point cabin, a palisade-log-cabin relic torn down over 20 years ago. The neighbors are still discovering items from

Dad's one time classmate and partner, Ed, forming an "original Ed" anthropological collection.

I am a Rememberer, but not just of family stories. I open the boathouse door and, through cellular memory, hook it to the outside post. I suspect Dad put it there so it would not blow shut and imprison the unsuspecting while getting fishing tackle from inside. I blow out candles when I leave a room. I bring in a few sticks of wood when passing by the wood pile, always replenishing the indoor cache.

I remember to blacken the stove, take out the ashes, but only after a few days of cooling. Once, I saw smoke rising from the corner of the garden's ash pile, another sign of Dad's then encroaching dementia. During those days, I remembered to check his whereabouts every 15 minutes. Even with that, I found him stuck, head hanging over the dock about to go into the lake, while trying to retrieve something among the rocks. Gratefully, his biceps were still strong enough at 85 to hold on until I got there.

I prefer to remember other days. Days when we sat under the full moon and threw bent candles into the fire, calling out the names of our dead, sending smoke messages into the universe. Our finite beliefs formed personal rituals, not necessarily in sync with Nature's laws.

Dad looked at his candle and said, "Death is a changing of the elements. The candle is solid in my hand. The wick can be lit and it gives off light. Over time, heat changes its solid form. It morphs, melts, exposes its wick. It burns down until there is only a puddle and then the flame goes out and the gasses rise up, mixing with the air. The entire candle still exists, but has passed through many forms and now, becomes one with the elements. It always was and will be part of the big picture, constantly changing."

Somehow, that was a comfort. Each candle represented love. Love survives. Every rock he moved, firewood he split, nails he hammered, was done out of love. His projects still exist. He is present when the breeze rustles shoreline grasses and the mother mallard leads her ten ducklings along the rock-wall he placed there to hold off erosion.

I am the Rememberer. I sit on this swing and watch thousands of sparkles dance on the lake. I will pump the water into the jug for lemonade. At 1:00 p.m., a young woman from last night's campfire will arrive at my trailhead. We will walk the high hills and circle around the valley where once people from Chicago used to bus in for skiing. It is local lore, a place she wants to discover.

I am the Rememberer. The ghosts will live again when I take her to walk the ruts of the ski hills and share their stories. Perhaps the hills will reveal the stories of those before me.

Greg Doth, in his own words
School Assignment

Greg
Doth
2nd hour

A place that has always been special to me would be my cabin in Wisconsin. Ever since I have been little, my mom has taken me with her to our cabin. It has always been a happy place and has always brought good memories.

The first time I visited the cabin, I was about 2 years old. I don't recall much except being bathed in a basin in the sink. I always ran around outside and went fishing with my Grandpa. Playing in the sandbox was also a favorite pastime of mine. I was always happy there, and never lonely, because someone would play with me all the time. Whether it be my mom, my Grandpa, or my Grandma, someone was always there to comfort

me or to lend me a hand.
I remember thinking that
my Grandma must be the
best cook in the world, because
everything she made always
tasted so good.

Now, when I visit the
cabin, it brings out the same
kind of excitement in me as
it did years ago. I still
enjoy fishing with my Grandpa
as much as I ever did. He
never ceases to amaze me with
how much he knows about
the subject. I still think
my Granma is the best cook
alive, as I have yet to taste
a better made meal. Every
year, when summer rolls around,
I look forward to our annual
trip to the cabin. I know
that I will have a lot of
fun, and that I'll also be
able to leave the troubles of
the "outside world" behind me.
I can be at peace with the
world and with myself, and
enjoy everything I do.

Epilogue

*"We do not inherit the earth from our ancestors,
we borrow it from our children.
We cannot simply think of our survival;
Each new generation is responsible to insure the
survival to the seventh generation ..."
- Chief Seattle
(Born circa 1780-86; Died June 7, 1866)*

My journey on this earth began in 1952. My parents took me to this remote parcel of the planet the following year, dipping my feet into the water, not realizing it as symbolic, a sacred baptism into the natural world.

These tales are to be retold around a campfire or a kitchen table. I've included writings of other family members, but only in the retelling will we share our story and our insights.

These stories are incomplete. They only hint at the multitude of trees cleared, tons (yes, tons) of rocks moved to terracing – some taken from the lake bottom, then by canoe to their embankment walls. The stories hint at interpersonal relationships, yet lack the struggles, the tensions, the deep grief, and long-term healing. Of course, there were long nights of the souls. There was handwringing involved, as well as Grandma Nellie's deep bosomed hugs.

My grandparents lived during the Great Depression, and, by necessity, recycled, reused, and repurposed way before that was a saying. After World War II, my parents' generation came into prosperity, with plastics and single-use products thrown into fields and streams of the "back 40." Ed's 1960s IH van still decays in a ditch on the Point. Even as my generation becomes enlightened to our collective responsibility for earth's health, we fall short of embracing ecology over ease. New facts demand new behaviors. Think seven generations.

Next steps: Looking back and learning from history

I want to learn about those people who walked these woods and canoed this lake before me. They were the Potawatomi. The Potawatomi still live in this region. Not surprisingly, the papers handed down to me depicted a history beginning with white men entering this land during their Civil War, constructing Military Road, logging, and the various railroads built through the marshes and woodlands to carry the downed forests to their mills.

Next steps: Looking to the future and leaving a legacy

It is imperative that I protect this parcel. I am pursuing a conservation easement. This land, the critters, and the future kidcos depend on us. I encourage us all to pursue ways to conserve, protect, and have best practices. Every personal habit, every pollinator plant, every patch of ground requires intentional attention. Beyond personal stories, I endeavor to protect the land.

Think seven generations out. Pass it on.

About the Author

Janet Kurtz was born to and raised by a United Church of Christ youth pastor and a third-grade teacher, both from small villages in northern Illinois. Roots ran deep in the culture of farm fields and trapping in the back creeks, Protestant work ethic, and empathy for the stranger in the land. These traits manifest in her lifelong career teaching Spanish and Latin American cultures, working with refugees, translation, and leading student travel study. Her first book is titled *Northern Shores/ Southern Borders: Revelations of a Bilingual Life*, in which she shares her own roots, planted in the woods of northern Wisconsin. Janet is most at home where the phoebe sings its name, the chipmunk fills its cheeks with pine nuts, the breezes whisper through the quaking aspen, and friends circle around a shoreline bonfire. These pages come from five generations of letters, journals, and essays, giving a collective glance into a Northwoods cabin... not a McMansion found on glossy pages of northern living magazines, but a real, vintage, honest-to-god cottage with a squeaky screen door.

·

www.ingramcontent.com/pod-product-compliance
Lightning Source LLC
Chambersburg PA
CBHW051616120626
46551CB00014B/1820